Fran and Her Friend Death

Fran and Her Friend Death

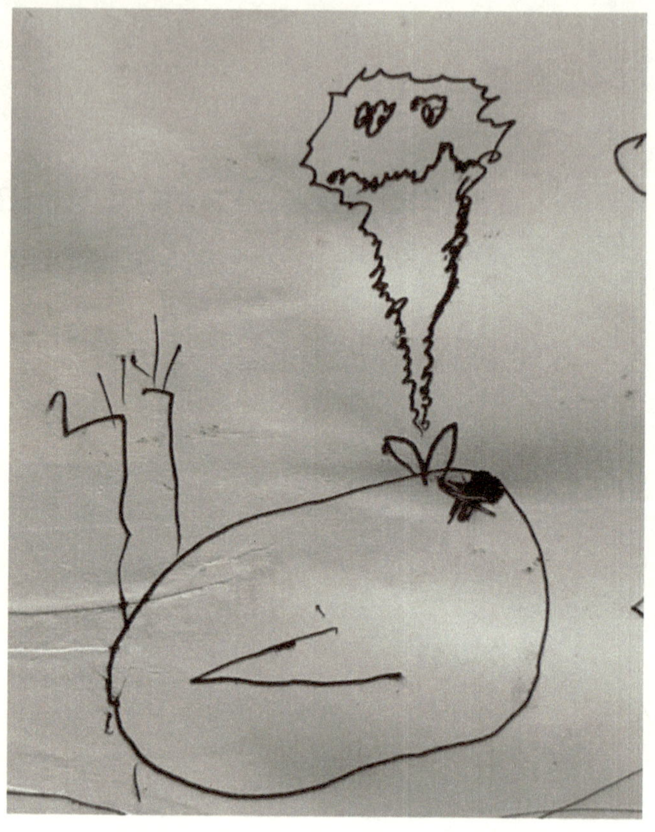

Special thanks to my wife, who had to try and decipher my chicken scratch when I was handwriting this on a notebook. To my son, Wyatt, who helped draw that bird up there that has a soul coming out of its beak, and Ryker and Sophia for being awesome cheerleaders. He's really excited to have his drawing on my book. A big thanks to my Dr. for helping medicate me with the appropriate attention medications. This one's for you, girl. Big thanks to stimulants. You know who you are, boo. I'd also like to thank the people who thought I could never get anything accomplished. Jokes on them. On paper, I looked like I'm actually accomplished. I made it! Sometimes. I still like my instant ramen noodles. Who am I kidding. I teeter totter between making it and not. Like a boss. I'd like to thank myself for being mentally unstable enough to see images in my head, and then writing them down for the world to see. Oh, and thanks to those who read it before this went live. Not many people did though. Come to think of it. I'm the only one who has read this book. I promise, it's an okay book. You will laugh at least one time. If it's hard to follow it, then I don't know what to tell you. I should open a fan email. If you have questions, or concerns, I guess you can email me at jdiegocervantes@icloud.com. If you want to be my literary agent, and have someone who can help me edit this for free, or low low cost, hit me up too.

<u>Note to the reader.</u>

This is my first book. It took me thirty-three years to muster the strength to sit in front of a screen for long enough to get anything typed. Full disclosure, I have no business writing a book. I did my best to write it and edited it. I know. There will be some typos and stuff. I'm not sure if I can fix it after I upload it, but I will try. If you buy my book, don't hate. I'm doing my best.

This book contains crude humor/language, commentary about religion some may find offensive (all in good humor). Read at your own discretion. All of the characters are fictitious. Any resemblance to anyone else is purely coincidental.

Table of Contents:

<u>Sucking at something is the first step to becoming sort of good at something.</u>

-Jake the dog

Fran and Her Friend

Death

J.D. Cervantes

Do Birds Have Souls?

Chapter 1:

Death lurked over a dead bird beside a tree. The sun was at its peak. It shined brightly across a large, black, empty asphalt parking lot that was littered with shopping carts strewn about nearly every single carless parking spot. A scraggly haired, strong body odored shopping cart attendant sat against his own car as he lit a cigarette with one hand and scoured the depths of Tik Tok with the other. He was overly proud of himself for the fact that he had just learned how to roll his own cigarettes, and he had one sitting against his lips to prove it. There existed virtually no sense of urgency within him to complete his job as he was hired to do so. Cart after cart, the parking lot became ever so littered with the tools that were needed by consumers to lug their groceries as the day progressed.

In the distance, a woman, presumably Death's intended target for the day, exited the grocery store the strewn about carts belonged to. He had been sent to that location with orders to collect the soul of a short old lady with graying, short bushy hair. However, he was given no specific time for which to expect her. Death soon found himself completely and utterly distracted by the sight of a poor, lifeless, little brown bird resting atop a mound of mulch that surrounded an oddly thick tree.

Death kneeled curiously beside the dead bird. Its brothers and sisters chirped restlessly about their day, and about how they saw Redmond (the dead bird) keel over and die mere moments before the arrival of Death. He looked at it as though he were contemplating whether to pick it up or not.

"Stop Messing around Redmond!" A bird chirped. He apparently wasn't aware that Redmond had just fallen out of his nest because of a massive rupture on his coronary artery. How could he have known though. The bird was no doctor, and he had not witnessed the fall in the first place.

"I think he's dead," Dayana chirped back. Dayana was the tree's biggest gossip. She always kept her beak in everyone else's business but her own. She flew down to Redmond's body to confirm, but Death's curiosity glued him to the small dead bird's body. He shoed her away with one swift flick of the wrist. "Rude!" she yelled. Death simply heard a beautiful bird singing a beautiful incomprehensible song being sung on a beautiful day. Dayana tried her luck and attempted to tug at Death's robe, but Edgar, the bird who was no doctor, also Dayana's spineless husband (her words), advised her not to do that.

"Hey!" he chirped at her. Death could swear he was listening to a lover's quarrel, or a love song between two birds hopelessly in love. "Don't do that Daya!"

Dayana very graciously chirped back, "mind your business honey! I can't let this guy do that to Redmond's dead body!"

"Redmond died? Edgar chirped. Seemingly, he was in shock. Dayana ignored him. "Do you have any idea who you're messing with?" he continued, choosing to leave the mourning for when they were a little farther from the grim reaper. Edgar flapped his wings quicker than the eye could see. He flew up to Dayana, careful not to get too close to Death and his beaten up, bloodied, rusty scythe. The stick on which it rested showed heavy signs of use and disrepair.

"This bozo? I have no clue who that guy is. I just know that he's desecrating our friend's body!" Dayana chirped away. "I'm trying to teach him a lesson!" This time she nipped at Death's hood. He patiently waved her off. His gaze remained locked on Redmond's body.

"Suit yourself, but I wanted to tell you that you're fucking with the grim reaper!" Edgar chirped. Dayana froze in her tracks, maintaining a stable hover just mere inches away from Death's head. He could feel the soft breeze coming from Dayana's rapidly flapping wings.

The shopping cart attendant considered, for just the briefest of moments, stepping away from his car to finally conduct the work he was being paid to do. With the greatest intention, he began the motion one does when one tries to move one's legs. A sort of half jerk, but not really. He even went as far as placing his phone back into his back pocket, which in hindsight would have been a mistake should he have continued doing the right thing on account of him having a massive hole ripped into it. He would regularly lose a plethora of items because he'd forget about the hole. Ultimately, though, he was powerless to fight against the gravitational pull of the comfort of his car. So, instead, he reached back for his phone, which was now on the verge of falling in through his torn pocket and struggled to have it recognize the pattern of his fingerprint. He tried once, but the phone could not recognize his dirty print. He tried twice, but now the phone was angry and threatened to lock up if he tried once against unsuccessfully, then picked at the deepest parts of his brain to remember his password. He input it carefully as failing to do so successfully would mean he'd lose access to his phone for at least a minute. After careful consideration, he tapped the screen doubtfully, but managed to unlock his phone. The home screen reflected brightly onto his pupils. Now with an air of success for his ability to remember his password correctly, he continued his quest for videos of small children falling from various slides of all shapes, or clips of kids running into walls of different textures.

Death's target, the senile old lady with cute, white bushy hair, and a tightly knitted grandma sweater she knitted during the long spans in between visits from her grown children, slowly opened the trunk of her black SUV that made her look ten times smaller than she really was. The SUV looked enormous in comparison. Her weak, saggy old great grandma muscles struggled with even the lightest of her grocery bags as she lifted them off of the shopping cart, and into the back of her vehicle. Her face reddened as she lifted each bag. She let out a long sigh of relief after achieving each of her tasks until every bag had been transferred over.

Death's phone pinged. An incoming text from God read, "Dude, what the hell?! Margaret, your target! Is about to leave! What in the world are you doing?" However, the message was left unread as Death reached for the nearest stick.

"Oh shit! he's getting serious!" Edgar chirped once he noticed that Death was probably reaching for a weapon, which was commonly known as his scythe.

"Wait Edgar! Don't leave me!" Dayana fluttered her tiny wings faster than she knew was possible. She flew behind Edgar in fear for her life.

Stick in hand, Death debated whether he should poke the dead bird or not. He'd never chaperoned a soul belonging to the animal kingdom in the past. A sudden gut punch like feeling took over him. He wondered if it had been his job all along to take the non-human souls, or if there was a specific department for different for inter-species affairs. If there were a different department, he'd certainly never seen anyone else doing the job. Fuck, have there been billions of upon billions of lost souls roaming across the vastness of earth that had been left unclaimed over the span of creation itself solely because of his ineptitude? The gut punch feeling into a much bigger feeling of nausea and shame. The voice within him that constituted what was considered his thinking voice grew louder, and it said, "you're an idiot."

He briefly removed his hood, revealing an orange, artificial glow from multiple vanity sessions under the UV light of a tanning bed, which emanated from his skull. He placed the hood back over his head after wiping off a bead of sweat that had accumulated on his brow. With a great amount of guilt, really more shame than anything else, he looked cautiously around him. He carefully made sure that God had not just witnessed him beyond royal level screw up. Because, let's face it, he most likely screwed up beyond any level of comprehension. The royalist of screw ups rested upon the hands of Death himself, and he was not about to let God find out about it. Once he felt as though God wasn't paying close attention (Death hoped that God had entrusted his intern to take over for a bit while he took a nap), Death took the stick he held tightly in his hand, zeroed in on the dead bird body, and poked the pre rigor mortis remains.

"What are you doing?" a soft, but confident feminine voice attacked him from behind. Death yelped a loud. His skittishness, and fear that he'd been caught had gotten the best of him. He shot up faster than springs being released abruptly after sustaining an enormous amount of tension for an enormous amount of time. In the distance, out in the parking lot, his target entered her car, and slowly drove off at the rate of speed that was painfully slow. She would later (not much later) single handedly cause bumper to bumper traffic at the height of rush hour. An accomplishment that normally took at least forty-five people to be involved in. Margaret was none the wiser from what nearly became her fate. She now owed the rest of her life, (For the second time. We will get to that part later.) in whole, to the likes of a dimwitted reaper who was too distracted to do his job due to a bird who had sadly recently become deceased. If Death were any other normal employee, in any other capacity, and in any other field, his ineptitude would have caused him to have been fired by now. However, due to the fact that Death was closely related to God (First cousin on his dad's side), God found himself unable to put an end to Death's atrocious career. God's parents were in the business of hiring a good ole nepotism hire, so, in all certain terms, Death was stuck being the reaper, and God was stuck employing someone who was incredibly bad at his job.

The shopping cart attendant decided he was too tired to complete the rest of his contracted duties. He also acknowledged how beautiful the day was turning into. The temperature around him was pleasant. The birds chirped happily, the clouds above him lacked, allowing the sun to shine brightly against what little exposed skin was exposed to. In short, the day was just too damn pleasant for hard labor, so he carefully assessed the level of effort he had to exert, and ultimately found that he had enough time for a quick little nap. The careless attendant opened the door to his black rusty, nineteen ninety dodge neon and stepped inside. The car lacked power windows, so he hand-rolled them down as low as they could. The back windows, unfortunately, only went halfway down. He was left breathless after he rolled the fourth set of windows down. Then, he reclined his seat to its lowest setting and zonked out. From the looks of it, it took him approximately point zero two five seconds to knock out cold. He let out an impressively loud, satisfying snore. His jaw fell open, allowing a glop of ooze like drool to slowly emerge from his gaping mouth. Both Death and his seemingly invisible accoster were impressed by the cart attendant's power to give absolutely zero fucks while at work, and more so at his ability to fall as quickly as he had.

In the meantime, Death froze after his dramatic jolt. He could not understand how it was possible for anyone else to direct any sort of communication toward him. Especially if that communication came from a human. He would understand if God were the one that, for some reason or another, had come down to reprimand him. However, he quickly remembered that God was in fact not a woman, and his voice was considerably deeper than that of the tiny voice he had just heard. His body grew tense. His muscles were now tighter than he'd ever felt them. Above him, Dayana chirped a series of expletives at him that are too inappropriate to be repeated in any language, animal or not. She chucked tiny branches at him, which registered as a normal occurrence resulting from the wind blowing against the tree branches, robbing Dayana's intended effect.

Death gulped. Slowly, he turned toward his female sounding aggressor. He let out a deep sigh of relief upon completing an about face and didn't see anyone standing behind him. His body softened in reassurance of not having been caught in a moment of monumental weakness. Mostly, he was happy that God had not caught him in the middle of what was most likely the biggest fuck up in the history of existence. He allowed himself to relieve some of the pent-up tension that had been building up on his shoulders.

A Ned Flanders looking man exited the grocery store. His face being the only Flanders like resemblance he had. The man towered over Death in comparison. He stood at a whopping seven and a half feet above the ground, and exactly a foot over Death. The guy was essentially made up of perfectly chiseled, marble, possibly granite boulders which gave him the appearance mirroring that of an Olympus God. If Death hadn't known any better, he would have certainly believed the man before him was in fact one of those Gods. The Flanders look alike would have been even more menacing if not for the fact that he wore a snug fitting green apron that covered the front half of his body, and a name tag with his title of manager accompanied by his name, Brody. The name itself deterred from the level of menacing vibes he could have given. Really it was a waste of potential, but he had his parents to blame for that. Brody scanned the parking lot carefully, in an obvious search for his cart attendant. Apparently, the store had run out of available shopping carts.

"Ehem" a voice half demanded Death's attention. He looked side to side. He thought he'd escaped the wrath of the feminine voice, only to feel a warm, frail (in the sense that the human body was naturally frail, because human. Not in in anyway because the incorporeal voice, so far, was anything resembling weak, or because it belonged to a woman.) finger gently poked at his chest. He looked down, investigating the developing nuisance.

"Well?" a slender woman of about exactly five feet in height followed up. Her neck bent backwards so as to attempt to make eye contact.

"What do you mean what am I doing?" Still, he remained unsure that he wasn't being set up. "Definitely not wondering if it's my job to claim non-human souls." He said. *Stupid, stupid. Why in the world would you say that. If that person didn't think that before, she definitely will now. She could have been sent down by the big guy!* He thought. He could not believe why he would have ever been possessed enough to admit such a thing.

"Meaning why are you poking at a dead bird. You're going to get dead bird disease, or something."

"Is that a thing?" Death asked. He now unlocked a new fear.

The small woman glared at the motionless bird. Then decided she didn't much care that Death was poking at a dead bird. There were plenty of other things she could choose to spend energy on, and that was not one of the things she could see herself spending energy on. So, she continued going on about her business as though she'd seen nothing quite out of the ordinary. Death looked at the bird, and then at the short annoying woman dressed in small, black short shorts and a nice-looking cat shirt riding a rainbow. Her clothing hugged her body just well enough to turn heads, but not too well so as to trigger any unwanted cat calls. Mostly, people were curious about the cat riding a rainbow on her shirt, but they all generally just kept to themselves.

"Hold on!" Death shouted. A short sprint allowed him to catch up to her. Brody locked onto the cart attendant's car. He walked up to it.

"I'm busy," the nosey woman dismissed Death as he approached. He struggled to catch his breath before remembering his lack or need of lungs. Regardless, he gasped for air.

"You can't just scare the shit out of me and walk away like that!" A pair of automatic sliding glass doors opened as they entered the building. Immediately, the smell of fresh produce inundated their nostrils, triggering a rather pleasant response worthy of having their mouth water. They were greeted, not by a geriatric greeter, but by the greenest of broccoli they'd ever laid eyes on as it sat beautifully on display. If it were a person, it would have been well aware at how delicious it looked, sitting there doing no more than just looking great. Despite the state of the exterior's apparent disrepair, the inside was nothing less than immaculate. The floor shined brightly without the trace of a single scuff mark. Apparently, their budget afforded them the liberty to both buff and wax the entire store on a regular basis. The lights from above gave the entire floor a sheen shine. It was as though the floor itself was emanating light, and not just serving as a reflective surface. As for the displays, everything from their shelves, candy towers, fridges and freezers were all stocked up with nothing but the most fresh and organic product available for public consumption. Not to mention the prices were reasonably priced. So much so that even the mysterious woman walking in front of Death was able to afford to shop there on a semi regular basis.

The woman shrugged. "Why not?" She asked in a way that conveyed how much she actually didn't care at all to continue her previous conversation. The curiosity she once had faded nearly as quickly as it had appeared. Now, she was on a mission, and frustrated that she couldn't find a single cart where one would normally be. "I guess I'm carrying everything," she mumbled to herself.

"Do you realize who you're talking to?" Death materialized he dented, well used scythe for added effect. It looked as though it may have been time to retire it, but he'd chosen to hold on to the thing because it had sentimental value, and that was something he couldn't get from a new scythe.

In the parking lot, Brody knocked carefully on the cart attendant's car door. A long strand of drool now reached his shoulder. It made Brody cringe. The radio played to the tune of wrecking ball by Miley Cyrus at nearly full volume. The speakers sounded as though they were about to die every time the music had too much bass.

"I'm pretty sure I know exactly who you are," she said. She remained completely unphased, immune to what his robe and his scythe had come to represent since basically the beginning of time.

"Does it not scare you that I am appearing before you?" Death made his best attempt to sound proper, and wise. His face failed to conceal that his feelings had been actually hurt by the lack of fear she displayed.

"Meh,"

"Meh? You must not really know who I am. Let me explain something." The woman before him placed her index finger gently upon his boney lips. Not out of anything sexy, but in an attempt to get him to stop talking. Death wondered where her hands had been recently. Had she washed them after going to the toilet? She shushed him the way a tired mom shushes a baby when she tries to put it asleep (not in the mean way, but the shh shh shh cute baby rocking type of way). She used her other hand to reach for a tub of gluten free, vanilla and chamomile tea ice-cream, thanks in large part to a recommendation her friend Cassandra had given her the night before. She had nothing but rave reviews. Likely, Cassandra had put so much weight into her colorful recommendation because she had just broken up with her boyfriend for the thirteenth time, and she used the ice-cream as a sort of comfort food while watching old reruns of Grey's Anatomy. Like season one old.

"Death. I know, big deal!" She removed her finger from Death's cold boney lips. "Do you know who I am?" She asked. Death struggled to keep up with her, both physically as she weaved in and out through maze like isles, and mentally. He had not had the capacity to keep up with her sass. He was thoroughly dumbfounded by the lack of fear he failed to instill upon her.

"Of course, I do."

Fran rounded the corner. By the time Death reached the end of the isle, she was already halfway down the opposite end of the store where they had a small section full of their clearance items. This left him wondering how in the hell it was possible for her to move so quickly without actually running. He took off in a sprint.

"Just to be sure, what's your name again?" he shouted from across the store. Breathing was suddenly harder now that he was actively running behind her.

"Mr., I know who you are. I've known you, or of you since my brain learned how to properly form any type of coherent memories. You were there when my grandma died. I used to see you coming in and out of the hospital where my mom worked. I even would catch glimpses of you at random car crashes along the highway. I used to think you were a family member since you were just about everywhere I was. Then I realized you never really gave us the light of day, except for when my grandma died. I was there when you invited her to follow you."

She grabbed a cookie pan. There were several stickers placed upon one another. They all had different prices printed on them. The most recent one showed the last markdown at ninety-nine cents.

Death flipped through a notebook containing the names of every single human that had every existed, is currently existing, and will most likely exist based on a very intricate algorithm his startup geek friend developed. He flipped through it.

"I don't have time for games, girl," he said with the most authoritative voice he could muster. The lights flickered around her. A sulfuric smell seeped out of nowhere. The skies above them rumbled loudly as lightning closely followed thunder. The world beyond the grocery store's walls became dark. The trees swayed violently from side to side as winds nearing speeds of up to a hundred and fifty miles per hour tested their ability to stay erect upon the land they'd learn to love. Brody even hopped into the back of the cart attendant's car. He abruptly, and very much frantically woke the attendant up as he barked orders to pull up the manual windows. They each shared frightful stares as they divided window rolling responsibilities. Edgar and Dayana, our noble, tiny bird-brained friends, braced for what appeared to be the imminent end of the world as they knew it. Death's chest puffed in a magnificent display of celestial toxicity.

"Relax, dude. I'm Fran. Quite frankly, I don't like your attitude," It was then that she decided it was not a good time to buy an unnecessary cookie pan. She placed it back neatly onto the shelf. A refurbished blender caught her eye.

Death's chest slowly deflated. The world around them immediately returned to normal, as if nothing had just happened. Brody noticed he was somehow now hugging his cart attendant tightly. He cleared his throat. They looked awkwardly at one another before letting go of each other.

Edgar and Dayana were not so fortunate. The storm was so mind bogglingly horrifying that it literally caused their hearts to explode violently within their chest. They now rested peacefully alongside their old friend, Redmond. A magnificent ornithological reaper appeared before both of their deceased bodies. Bird Death's wings were truly a magnificent, majestic sight to behold. They were long, and silky, and the blackest of blacks imaginable, which made for an unspeakably beautiful contrast against its bright white bones. His scythe (or hers, no one could really tell. It was hard enough to tell a normal bird's sex. It was even harder to figure out the sex of a skeleton. By that point, if you were nice about it, you were better off just asking. If it liked you, bird Death had no issue in sharing its gender/sex at birth. However, it didn't normally care to conform to any conventional gender. It liked to be more androgenous) was sharper, much shinier and in much better shape than the one assigned to the Death in charge of the humans.

Fran's Death, should he ever find out about the bird Death's newly upgraded scythe, was sure to release the full extent of his Karen like power upon HR if he felt that a bird had priority over him when it came to getting near gear. Luckily for the HR department, he was unaware of there being the need for anyone other than himself when it came to collecting the souls of earthbound beings. He unintentionally reserved his concerns about the lack of new equipment because he simply failed to realize there were more beings like him. If he were to have read his Reaper handbook, he would have realized that he was in fact not the only one who had been bestowed the job of aiding souls into the after-life. As far as he was concerned, he was the only Death, and he was not about to bitch about getting a new scythe when his career was on the line for having forgotten about the majority of earthly souls. Not that he felt the need for a new one. Nor did he realize he could request an upgrade.

Bird Death approached Edgar and Dayana's confused soul. "Come with me, my children, for you shall suffer no more." His voice was deep, but soothing.

"Do you always talk like that?" Dayana crossed her wings. Her hip popped to one side, the way a Karen does when she asks for the manager.

"Shut up, Daya!" Edgar pleaded nervously. He twiddled his wings out of a habit he developed from having to make Dayana back down from her many confrontations.

Human Death's target just narrowly escaped the brief apocalyptic deluge. The storm had just started as she brought the last of her groceries into her home. Somehow, she didn't notice a single thing out of the ordinary.

"How in God's earth are you not afraid of me?" He was beyond puzzled. In all honesty, he was hurt more than anything.

"Like I said. I've seen you around my entire life. At this point you're just creeping me out, like the annoying uncle who thinks he's really cool, but everyone else can tell he's just begging, no, crying for help because he'd developed a drug habit. The only thing you need now is to ask for a small loan. One that most certainly would not be repaid." She scoffed. The ice cream on her hands was beginning to make her fingers numb. They'd turned a light shade of purple.

"I don't understand. How can this be?" Death's tall, but by all means no taller, entirely less muscular and even less threatening frame than that of Brody's body became animated. "Do you know what these robes, this scythe, and the general skeletal body represent?" He swung the scythe around mightily. A loaf of bread fell off the shelf as he walked through the baked goods isle.

A disgruntled worker walked by just as the bread fell to the ground. His face was completely uninterested. Fran and Death could tell he wasn't dealing with any crap. He walked away.

Fran shrugged, as unamused as the grocery shop employee had just done so. She looked at the loaf of bread on the floor. "Are you going to pick that up?" She asked. Just like a wife that had just asked her husband to throw out the garbage, then waited exactly zero point zero seconds for her husband's dumb lizard brain to comprehend what had just been asked of him, she huffed in a display of displeasure. "Never mind. I'll do it." She leaned angrily over the loaf and tossed it back into its original spot. "Thanks." She glared at him.

"Man," she hissed. "You're no more scarier than a newborn little of cute puppies."

Death, on the other hand, was beginning to gain a small, but very real, level of fear toward her. He shook his head. *How can I be scared of such a small thing?* He thought.

"But how?" Death asked her. He fought through crowds of spaced-out grocery shoppers as he kept his pace beside her.

"I told you. You've been around me all my life. After a while it just becomes normal."

"That's even more of a reason to be afraid of me. You've seen what I can do!" Death's voice cracked as he pushed back a potential downpour of involuntary tears. He was not used to being disrespected this way. Most of the people who disrespected him at least had the decency to do this behind his back.

Fran looked at him from top to bottom. She stared at him for a good minute, or so. Random shoppers avoided her isle as it appeared as though she were staring and talking at nothing. They witnessed as she boomed her neck from floor to ceiling. A child and his mother walked by on the opposite end of the isle. The mother shrieked once she noticed Fran fighting with what was very visibly thin air. "This is why we don't do drugs, Mikey," she told her five-year-old son. He opened a bag of tortilla chips and spilled half of them at Fran's feet.

"Okay fine. You're soo scary," she conceded sarcastically. She even added an exaggerated shiver for added effect.

"Death raised a skeptical metaphorical eyebrow. "I don't appreciate being antagonized by a lesser being. By God, child, you will fear and respect me!" He commanded. Fran fake shook in fear again and walked away.

"Will that be all?" an over caffeinated cashier asked. Her voice was obnoxiously customer service like.

The smile on her face hid the please get me out of this hell hole feeling she had from the moment she set foot on the property. Her smile was big and welcoming. Her eyes told a different story. They screamed for someone to take her out of her misery. Death raised his scythe as though agreeing with her plea.

Fran looked over her shoulder. Reflexively, she threw a clenched fist into his gut as he was readying his swing the scythe. He frowned, then lowered his weapon. "What are you doing? "You're embarrassing me," she whispered harshly. The cashier threw her a dirty look as if to say who the hell are you talking to?

"Excuse me?" the cashier asked. Her face, while puzzled, remained indifferent. The only thing on her mind was what she wanted to eat for dinner.

"Oh, Nothing." Fran placed the ice cream on the conveyor belt. Death reached for a piece of candy, but she lodged her elbow into his chest for good measure. "I swear, you're worse than my nephew," Fran whispered.

Take It.

Chapter 2:

The Asian Market was more like a flea market. It wasn't an official establishment. The place most likely sprung as a result of a poor father selling fish out of his portable cooler in attempts to make an extra buck at the mouth of a seldomly used, industrial alleyway on the south side of Chicago. Business treated Wong very well from the get-go. Despite his traditional name, he was a native-born American who was raised in Chicago's own Chinatown. His parents were second generation American. Their Asian culture had been lost down the line in attempts to assimilate in a new country in order to be taking seriously. Everyone who bought fish from Wong would regularly assume that he was incapable of speaking English. Eventually, he got tired of it, and spent several months, and countless tiresome nights teaching himself how to speak Mandarin Chinese so that he could avoid talking to the racist assholes that automatically assumed he was too Asian to know how to speak the English language. His newly learned foreign language skills then made it so much easier to deny service to those who assumed he wasn't actually American.

Before long, another member of the Asian American community realized how profitable Wong's business was becoming. Having started with only one single cooler with fresh, quality fish, and expanding his operation by hiring contractors to build a small shack through which to sell his product within a matter of months, Wong inspired his friend, Lee, to open a shop of his own across from him at the mouth of said alleyway. Not wanting to be crushed by the competition, Lee invested in a thirty dollar, six-foot-long plastic table from his local hardware store. Without his wife's knowledge, he stole what few cooking pots and pans he could from her kitchen. Then, he borrowed his neighbor's gas stove he used for camping, and looked up an assortment of ramen noodle recipes until he landed on the perfect one so that he could offer it in his street kitchen across from Wong.

Just as Wong had, Lee quickly became profitable. His ramen noodles became the talk of the town. Conveniently, he used Wong's fish to add to his ramen menu, allowing each other to benefit nicely from one another. In similar fashion, more and more Asian American men and women discovered their niche. One street vendor turned into two, then three, and so on and so forth until the entire half a mile stretch of alleyway became saturated with now respectable vendors. This wonderful concoction of former poor men and women of Asian descent included one singular, shifty, short, and stubby Caucasian male in his mid-forties that went by the name of Frank Garillo. His small piece of the American dream rested in the center of the alleyway between a couple who had become the go to place to get a good roll of sushi, and a man by the name of Kyung Woo, who could fix just about anything that had a modern piece of technology in it. If he couldn't fix it, he'd find a way to do it, or help you find someone who did.

At the age of six, Kyung Woo had graduated high school with the highest of honors. MIT had even offered him a fully paid scholarship to whatever program he would choose from, but at the tender age of six, all he could think of was eating only the stuffing from the Oreo cookies his mom got him as a snack and taking a nap. MIT was beyond offended at his blatant transgression that they withdrew the offer all together.

Then there was Frank Garillo, a low-level conman who would do just about anything to make a dollar. He always wore a black fedora type hat, and garish looking shirts that were too small for his big arms and even bigger hanging belly. He almost always wore some variation of red and black striped pants that were two sizes too big for his short skinny legs.

Fran had a taste for delicious sushi. After her friend, Natasha, described how the near god like, celestial, soul crushingly delicious sushi Kim and Ho offered (Frank's commercial neighbor), she decided to check them out for herself, and so she did. Fran followed Natasha's directions cautiously. She felt out of place as the scenery went from neatly spaced-out households, and clearly defined city blocks, to that of a dirty industrial business district. She made sure to lock her car door as she drove by factories emitting large clouds of smoke into the formerly clean air.

There were several homeless people littering the sidewalks as they enjoyed the cool, overcast day around them. The weather app on her phone had not called for rain, but the grey clouds above them suggested there may be a storm brewing, unleashing a blanket of rain upon them at any moment. She continued in her search, strongly considering turning her car around, and settling for an instant cup of ramen noodles she had lots of in her pantry.

Just as she had decided to turn around, Fran drove past a busy alleyway crawling with people that walked in and out of it like busy bees. Whether they were going in, or coming out, they all had big bright smiles on their faces, specifically those that had concluded their visit because they'd most likely just enjoyed a good plate of some good food or another. The alleyway seemed as though it went on forever. It was difficult for her to see the end of it.

After finding a decent parking spot, which took the better part of thirty minutes, Fran finally weaved her way through the dense sea of people. It was like having to walk through a thick sea of sardines, it smelled like it too, while carefully avoiding unsolicited sales pitches from different salesmen, and women. They all shouted about their huge deals in attempts to lure their next potential customer. Most spoke in a language she did not understand but felt culturally insensitive at the thought of assuming it was Chinese. While it was effectively an Asian market, Chinese vendors were not the only ones occupying the space.

Busy bodies bumped against her unapologetically as she pushed her way forward. Her destination was now in sight, although her body felt as if she had just completed her first fight in fight club from simply walking in the alleyway.

As if from the shadows, a short man locked eyes with Fran as she neared Kim and Ho's sushi place. "Hey little girl," he said. It was hard to tell if the guy had a Jersey accent over the chitter chatter of a few hundred determined people. This, though, was the first English speaking white guy she had seen. Subconsciously, she felt relieved because his storefront was also the only one with signs in a language she easily recognized. His signs said things like, Frank's general store, and psychic readings-only twenty dollars per vision. Mostly, he sold questionably acquired items (many of whom believed they were stolen). He also duped people into believing he could speak directly to the dead. And, while he may have been lying about actually speaking to them, which he couldn't, he had an unnatural knack for being able to summon ghosts who were unable to cross into the afterlife.

Fran looked side to side. "Me?" She pantomimed while pointing at herself. *How likely is it that this guy randomly picked me out, out of the hundreds of people around me,* she thought. She walked closer to him, unable to resist his cunning lure. He grabbed her arm the moment she was within reach, and escorted her closer toward his place of business, which was essentially nothing more than a retired circus tent affixed upon a semi-permanent commercial landscape.

"Please, step inside," Frank told her. His grubby fingers no longer held her arm. He didn't want to appear too aggressive.

The inside of the tent was dark. The room, or space, was filled with the smell of cheap incense. A few makeshift displays littered the floor. They all had tacky tablecloths on which his products sat. Some displays show cased gaming systems, like the very first Gameboys, or Playstations. Other displays were nothing more than old, discarded scientific calculators, and brick like Nokia cellphones that had collected layers upon layers of dust. The whole place couldn't have been too sanitary. She feared that visiting for too long would cause her to acquire a terminal disease. Regardless of the potential health complications she may experience because of her patronage, Fran felt an obligation to properly window shop. Her stomach growled, but she was in too deep, and the thought of excusing herself felt as though it were too much effort.

At the center of the tent there was a large pole which held up the structure. On it hung a variety of shriveled shrunken heads of all different species. She had a strong suspicion that one of them may have even been human, but she chose to believe that it was fake for the sake of her sanity, and not have to testify about it in court.

"I shrank those myself," Frank said. His voice was deep and gruff, and much more understandable now that it wasn't competing against the voices of a million other people. It gave her the impression that he had been a smoker for most of his life. His hands clasped together. It looked as though he were washing his hands, or possibly plotting her murder.

Fran explored the rest of the tent, which was larger on the inside than it looked from the outside. It gave her a funny feeling that she had stepped foot into a ghetto Tardis.

"See anything you like?" He pointed at a display of cheap, knock off purses. Fran glanced at the briefly out of politeness, then shook her head.

"How about those state-of-the-art Ouija boards?" He pointed, then ran toward the table they sat on. The boards were the only ones that seemed to be truly authentic out of the collection of knick knacks he had just offered her. It caught her attention, though. She bee lined straight toward it, narrowly avoiding tripping over a bear carpet. Literally, a carpet made of bear skin. The only thing missing was the bear head, but he had to remove it due to strict customs regulations that banned the transportation of endangered species across national lines. He is yet to disclose exactly where, or how he'd gotten the bear skin. Anyway, he managed to avoid a hefty fine while crossing into the U.S border by removing the bear's head, which made it virtually impossible to prove the animal he'd killed was in fact endangered. He did, however, have to deal with an interrogation inside a small room, no bigger than four feet by six feet, and a slap on the wrist.

"This board here was recovered from a house dating all the way back to the Salem witch trials." He gasped for air in between words. His breathlessness confirmed the idea Fran had about him being a lifetime smoker. Beads of sweat formed above his brow. His loud red shirt revealed a rapidly forming sweat stain under his pits. She was hooked.

Frank handed her the board. There was considerable weightiness to it. The wood was sturdy and looked real. Unlike the cheap, mass-produced versions she'd occasionally see at the stores. Several small cracks and ridges decorated the old dry wood, giving it the feeling of it being at least a couple hundred years old. There were no signs of it ever having been refurbished in any way. The letters were carefully etched, and not with a modern-day router. She could notice where the imperfections rested after whoever crafted it carefully placed his or her chisel, then pounded it against the wood with a careful swing of a hammer. Then, to finish the creepy effect, the indents that formed the letters were perpetually dyed with the help of some sort of flame that carefully drew within where it was intended, and nowhere else. Whoever made this Ouija board was meticulous about every detail that went into crafting it. Fran's eyes widened.

Frank honed in on his opportunity. "Legend has it, the board used to belong to Elizabeth Howe back during the trials." Fran was unable to avert her gaze. She looked at it the way a new mother looked at the infant that had just come out of her. Her breathing shallowed. She stood in amazement and nodded as Frank spoke. Rumbling from her stomach interrupted his story. He looked at her, asking if she was going to take care of that with only his eyes. She shook her head. Frank continued. "Elizabeth was accused of afflicting a poor man's daughter, along with some of their livestock. For this, the woman was hanged. Apparently, her and her friends, Rebecca, an elderly nurse beloved by all, Sara Argood, a poor, destitute homeless beggar, Susanna Martin, an impoverished widow and Sarah Wildes, a newly retired lady accused of adultery, would all convene regularly when the moon was at its most full and practice their witchery.

The lights within the tent began to dim. A cold chill ran down Fran's small frame, which began from the nape of her neck and ran down the length of her spine. She squeezed the Ouija board closely against her chest. She could have sworn the temperature inside had dropped considerably since she'd stepped in. Suddenly, she felt a soft, warm, fuzzy thing rubbing against her slowly. Fran stood still. She now had justification for feeling an ominous energy running down her spine. "Meow!" Meowed a cat from beneath the display table. The cat, who Fran will later come to know as Catgatha, blinked the slowest blink at her. She purred in pure bliss at receiving any amount of attention from Frank's visitor.

"Oh, hi kitty!" Fran said, averting her gaze from the board for just long enough to squat down, and put the kitty.

Frank paused. He reached for the planchette while his would be customer took a moment to get the petting out of her system. The planchette was equally as breathtaking as the board it was paired with. There was no doubt in her mind that it was the real deal. There was a spider-web crack in the middle of the glass that would be used to hover over

the letters that aided with communication with the spirit
realm.

"The group of women would use their time together
to summon all manner of demons in order to do their
bidding," Frank continued with the story. He took a good
look at the planchette, placing it over his eye so that it
would become distorted on Fran's side. His eye multiplied
into as many sections as the spiderweb crack created. A soft
gasp escaped from Fran's lips, not at the mutant looking
eye, but at the idea of the feisty five (a name she thought fit
for a group of badass women who went against the grain in
a time when people were dumb-er) group of women
coming together and bitching about the assholes in her
town. She was fairly certain they weren't witches.
However, come to think of it, the idea of witches wasn't all
that implausible now that she had met Death. If he was real,
witches roaming the streets sounded like an entirely
plausible reality. She covered her mouth with her free hand
to conceal her gasp, carefully making sure not to drop the
Ouija board as she pried herself away from the cat.

"How do you know those women actually did that?"
the words were muffled because of her hand. Somehow,
Frank understood.

"I'm also a medium," he told her. Frank took the board from her. He placed it back down, then moved his arms around in a motion that more or less said follow me. "Unfortunately, the board is not for sale." The news was visibly devastating to Fran. Her entire evening's plans would now have to be re-planned. "What I can do for you, though" he continued, "is help you connect with someone in the afterlife.

"Sounds pretty vague. Just anyone?" She raised a brow. Although she was one hundred percent on board now due to the rush of adrenaline she got from the Ouija board, she refused to show him all her cards. She didn't want to look like an easy person to fool.

"I can't make specific people show up. It doesn't work that way. Usually, it's someone that's close to you in some way. It could be a family member, a teacher, or maybe even an old creeper that died and remains obsessed with you even in death."

"What's that going to cost me?" This was the part she was waiting for. This is where she expected him to try and milk her dry. Fran was ready to reel him in. Make him feel like he was going to make a good sale, then rip the rug from under her at the last moment and say something profound, like nah.

"That's the thing. I don't want your money." He told her.

Fran got real pervy vibes from him at that exact moment. She stepped away from him just a touch. "I'm not going to have sex with you," she said. Her face was disgusted. She couldn't believe he'd even think that was a real possibility.

"No! nothing like that!" Frank said. He took a few steps away from her, closer to his psychic table near the rear of the tent in a demonstration of how harmless, and not pervy he was.

Fran looked at him with a growing amount of doubt in her eyes. She rubbed her left elbow with her right hand. She wondered if she was about to have to use the mace she bought at the gas stations solely because it looked cute, and it was pink. She then wondered why she'd like something so colorful when her wardrobe consisted of nothing but black clothing, minus a few items that were embarrassingly colorful. She vowed never to allow anyone except for the inside of her room to see her so indecent.

He could tell she was becoming uncomfortable, so he bypassed the shtick he had about souls, and went on with it. "I was just going to ask for your soul," he said.

She remained a bit put off. If the Ouija board was truly authentic, though, certainly then would he be a man to be trusted. At least to some extent. "Just my soul?" she asked.

Frank nodded. He pulled out a chair that sat next to a small round table with a tacky red (velvet looking, but not quite) that was chilling under a dimly lit spotlight. She spotted Catgatha sitting on a dresser-looking object behind the table. She gave her fur a quick licking, then fell asleep. Frank pointed at the seat in front of him. He hadn't moved since pulling the chair out for her. She considered her options. If she wasn't allowed to purchase the most awesome looking, demon summoning, Blair Witch Project, Salem Witch Trials Ouija board that could have potentially changed her life and traumatized her in more ways than she could ever imagine, she was going to trust Frank not to have hidden cameras stacked around the tent waiting for her to take her clothes off and somehow end on a sketchy porn website later that evening.

"I'm in," she said with a toothy grin as she approached the chair that was being held by Frank's grubby, chubby fingers. His knuckles had a thick coat of hair that ran almost down to his cuticles. He wore no wedding ring but did have a collection of heavy looking gold rings on every other finger. Frank helped her scoot the chair in once she sat. He was surprisingly very professional.

"This is what I need you to say," he advised. Fran nodded. She could feel an odd sense of excitement. As long as he wasn't playing the long game, and really, he expected her to start being sexy at any point. Frank reached for her hands. "Please, place your palms upon mine."

A thin sheet of fog began to hug the table. *This is so cheesy,* she thought. Without being too obvious, she looked for a fog machine as the thin sheet of fog slowly turned into a thick blanket cloud formed above the table. It sort of leaked onto the floor. Fran placed her palms on Frank's.

"Are you ready?" He asked. Fran nodded. Her palms were sweaty. "Repeat after me." She did as he asked. "I hereby renounce any rights to my soul, and gift it onto thee, Frank Ulysees Garillo," Fran giggled after hearing the name Ulysees. She didn't the name fit. Frank continued despite her interruption, "henceforth and forever within the confines of perpetuity and thereafter. As God as my one and only witness. This holding of hands being legally binding in both the earthly world, and the celestial realm most know as the afterlife. Both in American law, and in the astral law. This contract can and will not be dissolved for any reason, albeit reasonable or not."

"You're going to have to slow down a bit, dude."

Meanwhile, a ghost cozily rested upon an exceedingly old, and even more comfortable vintage gray chair within the confines of Fran's room. The ghost had just picked up his favorite novel. He was about to read it for the thirty second time since her book collection wasn't extensive. It was more like a pile of books thrown about the room that she had promised herself to read in her downtime. Then when her downtime came about, she'd forget about them and turn to her reality shows instead. The ghost had even taken his time to make himself a good hot chocolate. A delicacy we were normally not privy to as Fran despite chocolate, especially the hot kind. Well, she really didn't like dark chocolates. She was more of a white chocolate type of person. He rested his hot sugary drink atop a cute little side table she had recently found and purchased for a total of five dollars at her local goodwill. She knew that they were simply taking shit for free from people, and marking it up, but she felt as though she was truly helping her community by buying from them. That, and their prices were pretty good considering their items were all used and abused. She'd had the side table appraised shortly after having bought it because something about it told her it may have been worth more than it seemed. Sure enough, the appraiser informed her that it was worth at least twelve thousand dollars, and if she had its identical counterpart, she could have sold the pair for more than double. The auctioneers, and the auctioneering organization would of course have had to take their twenty five percent cut, each, so really, she wouldn't have been much better off. Instead, she'd chosen to keep her single side table. She believed it helped her room feel more cozy. More her style. Quaint, mostly broken, yet still functional. The ghost was eager to take a sip of his brown, sugary beverage. He was excited to eat the marshmallows swimming on its surface as they filled with hot chocolate. He even remembered to place a coaster under his drink this time, after having to deal with Fran's groaning about where in the hell the liquid ring stains were coming from. Then, without warning, he disappeared.

Back at the tent, Fran sat with her eyes closed across from Frank. "Open your eyes," he said.

Fran opened her eyes slowly. The light, although dimly lit, hurt her eyes until they were able to adjust. Slowly, the silhouette of another person appeared sitting on the table. "Who the hell is this guy?" she asked.

I Can't Remember.

Chapter 3:

"I can't remember" Fan said. Her tone showed no signs of belonging to anything other than a generic, lifeless AI program. She sat alone in her softly lit room, on an old reclining chair that used to belong to her great grandfather, whom had, at the time, acquired it from an estate sale. The only light around her belonged to that of her computer monitor's save screen. It shuffled through random pictures for her recent, and not so recent adventures. Most of the pictures were of beautiful foreign landscapes with only one person in them as she held the phone in front of her. Fran, it was Fran. They were selfies of her in different countries.

"What do you mean you don't remember," a faint, ominous voice whispered, no, growled in a manner so guttural and horrifying that would cause anyone's heart to skip a beat. The voice gave one the feeling that it was hostile, and surely not one to be messed with. It was menacing to the degree that it would make even the strongest of strong men tremble where they stood. The voice itself came from nowhere, and everywhere at once. It was a thing nightmares were made of.

"Up until now, I thought souls were a made-up concept," She replied, completely unphased by the nightmarish, ominous voice. Her tone remained level, almost monotone and disinterested, more so inconvenienced. "How is this a problem?" She asked. The room around her became frigid, despite programing her thermostat in a way that kept her apartment at a comfortable seventy-two degrees, and the only window in the room having been tightly shut. A disconcerting breeze caused the ambient temperature all around her to drop by about forty degrees, or so it felt. It was enough for her breath to become visible upon everyone her of exhalations. She remained thoroughly unmoved with the developing situation. It was almost as though this was not the first time something like this had happened within the confines of her room. She simply stood from the comfort of her grey vintage chair (which she was almost a hundred percent certain of it being haunted, on account of having seen it rock back and forth on its own on more than one occasion,) and casually walked to her closet to grab a more suitable outfit considering how cold it now was.

She looked through her closet, which was home to an extraordinary collection of clothes ranging in all sorts of shades of black and gray. Fran shuffled through a wide selection of warm wear, finally deciding on an oversized jet-black hoodie she'd bought off of a clearance rack at a second hand store no more than three or four weeks prior. This was the first time she had chosen to wear it, besides the one time at the store when she was trying it on.

"Everyone has one, Fran," The deep, growl-like voice now sounded more irate, and even more hostile than before. It was as though had somehow insulted the voice, or his mom. Her confession of both not remembering where her soul was, or that she believed it wasn't real, deeply angered the unseen, commanding voice.

"Look, dude," she said as she put the large sweater over her spaghetti strap tank top, which happened to be pink. She wasn't completely devoid of owning anything with color. She just chose not to wear it in public. The air around her shifted as if there were a solid figure pacing beside her. "Some guy told me he could read my fortune and let me talk to dead people. All I had to do was give him my soul, so I did. It wasn't anything official, or anything. He had me repeat some stupid thing after him."

"I'm not sure what you mean."

"Something about giving him my soul for the rest of eternity here on earth, and in the celestial plane."

"And you just, gave it away. Just like that?"

"Pretty much. The lights flickered a little bit. Then I saw some ghostly figure on top of a small table with a horrible tablecloth. I figured it was some type of projection.

"What guy? What? Where?" He was more confused than ever.

"I was a little creeped out at first, not going to lie, but it turned out okay. I was mostly afraid of ending up on some shitty porn site," she explained. "If you're going to yell at me, the least you could do is come out, you wimp." Fran debated on whether to wear a pair of sweatpants, or deal with Death's incessant need to turn up his personal air conditioner he kept at below freezing levels wherever he went.

"That's no way to talk to a celestial being," Death's voice softened. His voice now sounded as it normally did. More human, and much less confident and commanding of blind obedience. He sounded like his feelings had just been hurt more than anything.

Fran chose to grab the warmest pair of pants she owned. The type people would normally wear when they go snowboarding, or when they climb Mount Everest.

"You don't have to be so dramatic. It's not that cold in here." Death said in response to her choice in outerwear. The air around him looked as if he were in a giant freezer though.

"Post menopausal baby," she shot back. Death materialized where the cold fog was accumulating. He glared at her from behind his hood.

"I told you. I run hot."

"Whatever. Sally." Fran teased. "To answer your question, some short chubby dude with black and red striped pants two sizes too big for him stopped me while I was out looking for a good roll of sushi over at the Asian market. He had the cutest black cat named Catgatha." Her face lit up. "Too bad I couldn't steal it."

Death folded his arms. Not in disbelief, because that's something he would expect from her, but more so in disappointment. Fran knew she was allergic to cats, yet she considered robbing a man (a shady one) from his companion.

"One thing led to another, and there I was, giving him my soul."

Death walked over to the light dimmer next to her door. He turned the dial as far right as it went, in turn then brightened Fran's room as much as possible. She covered her eyes at the onslaught of light that was now penetrating her eyes. It was as though her optical nerves were being attacked at every angle by a group of tiny little light knights, all holding bright metallic reflectors in order to render her essentially blind, and that she was blinded temporarily by Death's inconsiderate need to illuminate his surroundings. She hissed at him while her pupils constricted enough to fend off the surge in photons that now occupied her room.

"What is wrong with you!" She cried while uncovering her eyes, slowly. Very, very slowly. "I hate you so much more now," Fran said.

Death looked through her drawers, seemingly looking for any indication that her soul hadn't actually been detached from her body. "So now what? What if you die and you don't have your soul?"

"I dunno," Fran shrugged.

The reaper walked away from the drawer. He left every drawer open as he made his way toward her computer monitor. "Did you really give the guy your soul?" He refused to believe the transgression."

"Yes. I really gave him my soul. I didn't even feel anything."

He took a moment to process the information, but not before he woke up her computer so that he could check his myspace.

Fran slapped the computer mouse away from his cold, boney hand. He looked at her with bemusement.

"I'm going to pretend you're just being your regular pain in the ass self and assume that you're joking, or flat out trying to get under my skin.

"What skin?" She asked.

He rubbed the sting that lingered on his hand after Fran smacked it. "Do you have any idea what goes into making a soul? Or what a soul is even worth?" he asked as he gently rubbed his temples. Although he lacked any conceivable respiratory system, his breaths increased as though he were on the verge of hyperventilating. The abhorrent attack on his wrist was now a distant memory. He was not to forget about the blatant attack of such severity so easily though. He'd get her back for that later. The imminent panic attack he felt was a result of Fran's carelessness, and utter disregard for the safety of a sacred soul. The very thing he was created for had been recklessly discarded as though it were just any piece of painfully normal garbage. Fran was a danger to society in more than just one realm.

Fran's face presented an intentional lack of interest. Instead, she turned her attention to her computer, pushing Death aside with one forceful pop of her hip. The screen displayed a picture of Death's face on his myspace profile. His appearance was not much different than it was in real life. The biggest difference being that his skeleton looked more youthful, and brighter. He didn't have an orange hue yet because he hadn't discovered the glorious tanning bed studios. Surprisingly, he even looked skinnier then than he does now.

"I was under the impression that a soul was just something that crazy religious nut jobs made up to scare people into submission." She scrolled onto the next picture in his profile. This one was a picture of him not wearing a shirt. He had photoshopped an impressive six pack over where his, well, bones would normally be. "Also, you're trying too hard. Who uses myspace? And, who in their right mind is going to believe you have a six pack?"

Death snapped his fingers, making the computer shut off. "This is private," he said.

"Well then," he continued, then took a seat on her vintage chair. Death brushed something off and whispered something inaudible. Fran assumed that he was fighting with the chair ghost she thought haunted it. Death crossed one leg over the other, being careful not to let his robe ride up and expose his boney orange spray tanned legs. "I bet if you knew how much your soul was you wouldn't have given it away. I'd feel really dumb if I were you."
He elongated the word "real" for effect but did nothing to stir a reaction from Fran.

Her interest was piqued. "What do you mean my soul specifically? Are some souls worth more than others?" She asked. Fran overlooked the rolling, ergonomic rolling desk chair, and sat on the rickety Walmart brand desk itself. To her defense, the desk had been on sale and was the only one she could afford at the time without having to resort to living off of instant ramen noodles for the rest of the week as a result of her purchase. Just as most Americans, she was shackled to the biweekly meager earnings that her paycheck reflected, and she had just under a week to go before she didn't have to choose between starving or buying basic necessities. Albeit the desk wasn't a pressing matter. She just really, really wanted it. Especially because it was seventy five percent off, and up until that point she had used a pile of old crates and stacked them into a makeshift desk. It was rather difficult having to navigate her old-style rollie ball mouse over the uneven surface of the crates. Also just like most Americans, she was incapable of passing up such a good deal despite the fact that it would mean she'd have to forego more substantial nutrients or paying her rent on time.

"It depends on the person, really." He materialized a chalice out of nowhere. It dripped an unnatural green goop that turned into a toxic looking green mist as it traveled further down its bright gold ridges.

"Mine's probably not worth much then. I'm a non-believer of the celestials," she said. Although it felt more like she was mocking him. She emphasized the word celestial sarcastically, which should have been a pretty good indicator of her mockery. Death glared at her.

"So, fuck me then, right?"

"Yeah, pretty much." Her feet dangled from the desk. Death hoped that it would crumble beneath her as her legs kicked back and forth. The snow pants created a dry rubbing sound every time her legs moved.

"Funny," Death said. He turned his head slightly left and up toward the ceiling. "I'm technically considered to be a celestial. Let me tell you. God is a party animal!" He chuckled.

Fran's attention was now diverted to her phone. One of her annoying friends had just come into town and was texting to see if she could meet up for a margarita. She weighed her options. The morning was still young, but she decided to take a pass on the offer on account of having twenty dollars left in her bank account.

"The things the guy did when he was in his female phase. Well, I guess she at the time."

Fran's phone vibrated for nearly three consecutive minutes. All texts from her friend who was trying to get day drunk, and cat call hot dads wearing gray sweatpants.

"She was the one who taught me what a butt chug was back when I still had flesh. Come to think of it, she invented the butt chug. It started more as a question when she got stoned with me and the devil one night. "Dude, do you think we can chug a beer with our butt?" she asked. I was so high I started getting paranoid. I thought my arms were getting longer."

"So, God is real, and he used to be a bad bitch?" Fran asked.

"Well, yes. Also, no." Death replied.

"I don't get it."

"For starters, he's tired of people praying to him. He thinks those people are a bunch of lazy asses that are too unmotivated, and way to willing to let their lives rest on the hands of someone else."

"I could have told you that."

"Second of all, I've seen his mail room He never actually looks at any of those prayers. He lets them pile up, then has his unpaid intern shred them when he starts feeling like a hoarder." Death takes a sip of his radioactive looking drink. Then places the chalice on the floor next to his chair. He looks to his left as if to warn the chair ghost not to spill his drink. He points his finger at nothing. At least not anything Fran could see.

"God sounds like a real Gem. How are you a celestial?"

"I was chosen by God to kill the people he doesn't like, or those that are too old, or the ones that serve no purpose in society, or" he continued on with a long list composed of basically everyone.

"So, everyone?"

"Yeah, pretty much. There's really no rhyme or reason to it. I just follow orders. Also, we are biological family."

"That's what they said during the holocaust. Not the family part," She clarified.

"Fucked up, isn't it?"

"So, about this soul thing. How do you determine which ones are worth more than others?"

"Religious people are generally worth the least." The breaking news takes Fran by surprise.

"Why?"

"Our researchers found that most of religious people are the ones that cause the most harm." She nodded in agreement. Her level of attention to someone else's words is unlike anything she'd ever done before. She was by far the most attentive had ever been.

"I knew it! I want to hear why they think so though." She leaned forward and placed her hands on her chin to indicate how intently she was listening.

"Think about it, Fran." Death takes on a more professorial posture. Fran eats his every word. "Who else leads armies of people to kill other people in the name of their God?"

"Religious people!" She blurts out confidently. Her sentiment about religion had now been confirmed. This newfound information drowns her endorphins, making her forget about the bleak financial situation she was in. "This all tracks." Surprisingly, she wasn't being sarcastic or dismissive.

Death summoned a Cuban cigar. He lit it. Fran was briefly taken aback by this, but she let it go as long as he could produce one for her as well. She didn't want to smoke it. What she wanted to do was hold it and pretend to take a puff like they did in the old black and white movies. Death materialized another hefty cigar and handed it to Fran.

"He especially hates the people who don't miss a day of church. Weekend? I'm not sure when they actually do their thing. Anyway, he loathes the guys that claim to be righteous. Then they go home and beat their spouses or harass a poor black (insert whatever other minority population here) or gay guys in the name of God.

"Hallelujah. I feel so validated." Fran is now on the literal edge of her desk. Her baggy apparel seemingly melting off of her. Not really melting, more so she looked like a black pile of something with a head that was sitting on a creaky desk, but gave the impression that she was melting.

"Yeah, those guys are worthless. Bunch of son's a bitches." Death was disgusted.

"I thought you had to be impartial."

"I'm not impartial. I have the right to hate people just as much as you do. I just can't pick and choose who I help cross over to the afterlife."

"Makes sense. Who'da thunk," she followed. Although she somewhat expected religious assholes being hated by God just as much as she hated them, she wasn't expecting her sentiment to be anywhere remotely how he actually felt about them.

"Oddly, nuns are worth a pretty penny. At least the good ones. You know, with the whole catholic priest thing. I really thought they would be in on it."

"This also tracks. Look at Mother Theresa."

"Oh, no. Not her. She's the Devil's secretary. Can't tell you why, but I think she's being replaced by someone else soon."

"Please tell me that Betty White was a good person, and that her soul was worth at least a billion dollars. I know she wasn't a nun, but still."

"It wasn't worth a billion dollars, but she was cool." Fran let out a thankful sigh.

"Then there were the gays." Death continued. "Those guys have expensive souls. At least the ones here on earth. When it comes to other dimensions, or other worlds within our dimension, they are about average. They are only worth more here on earth because of the hate and discrimination they are forced to suffer through. On earth, their soul can be worth a million dollars, hands down." Fran's jaw dropped. "Non-monetary value, it translates into just about a fifty fifty chance of getting into heaven. If you ask me, that's a pretty good deal considering most everyone else has to make their way up from the base of zero percent. They get their advantage solely because they have more to deal with than the average person, like unjustified persecution, ridicule during their youth. You know, all the normal shit they must live through because people are generally garbage."

Fran nodded again. She figured it sounds pretty fair considering having bared witness to one of her friends as she suffered through an unforeseen hate crime on more than one occasion. Georgiana, her lovely lesbian lifetime friend, regularly had to suffer through harassment, discrimination, and violence entirely because of her choice in genitals. Despite her unfortunate circumstance, Fran had never met, or heard of, anyone kinder than her (Except for Mr.Beast, some random youtuber who helped people all over the world).

"Wait," she stops Death before he can utter another word. "The part of monetary value. You're telling me I could have sold my soul for cold hard cash?" Death shrugs his shoulders.

"You never asked." He takes another sip of his goopy green ooze drink, then gulps it down dramatically.

"I'm behind on every one of my bills. Meanwhile, I could have been raking it in? provided my shitty soul was worth anything." She motioned as though she were making it rain.

"Ten million earth dollars, if I remember correctly," Death says. He slaps an invisible hand away from his drink, then shoots a death stare at it as if to say *try it again and I'll erase you from every single realm in existence.*

Fran's jaw met the floor. Her eyes widened to the size of extra-large pepperoni pizzas. She tried to speak, but her body refused to produce any sounds remotely resembling that of the English language. Instead, a series of short, high pitches squeals and squeaks, and ums and uhs escaped from within the deepest corners of her lungs. Death looked at her twitch and glitch in amusement. He looked to his left. "Right? Why would she have done something so stupid like that?" This time, his conversation with the ghost was audible. He turned his attention back to Fran. "Remember to breathe," he reminded her. "I don't want to have to collect you any earlier than I have to. Especially now that you don't have a soul. You've got a decent number of miles left in you," he said.

After about a minute, maybe a minute and a half, just long enough to cause a high degree of dizziness nearing black out, but not long enough to cause any considerable brain damage, Fran's lungs began to spasm, begging her for a fresh gulp of fresh oxygen. She took a deep breath. Sort of like the ones people do when they've been under water too long and managed to resurface just in the nick of time. The once rapidly fading colors from her face found themselves creeping their way back, which gave Fran's cheeks a rosy looking color.

"You're telling me, the brokest of broke girls, that I could have been living it up, shopping at Nordstrom Rack instead of Ross's this entire time?!" She flailed her arms erratically at nothing. Death couldn't help but compare her to an image of a chicken running around without a head, which he'd seen at least once or twice. "What good is a soul for anyway? And why is it worth so much? I don't even believe in God, or religion. If anything, I talk shit about it all the time!"

Death bickered with the chair ghost. Apparently, the roaming spirit had grown a keen fondness to the chair, and wanted Death to move so that he could once again rest its ghastly ass on it. If Death was known for anything, though, he was not known to be one to back down for anyone, except for his mom, or God, or the Devil, or Life (he never understood why she was so upbeat all the time), or Fran when she's hungry. God's personal lacky was not about to concede to Casper. Luckily for the ghost chair, Death had forgotten his purpose, so being God's muscle meant nothing to the lost soul. Death wasn't too worried about seeing a soul that hadn't crossed. He was even less concerned with trying to help him move on to the afterlife. Mostly because he'd enlisted the help of a startup geek from San Francisco to come up with a program that would automate the soul reaping (he was more like a chaperone) process. At the moment, there was still a bug or two that needed to be fixed. Being the understanding celestial that he was, Death found it within himself to cut the startup geek some slack because he had just graduated from some online university, so he was still learning the ropes. Had Death known any better, he would have gotten a sneaky suspicion that the startup geek was in fact slacking. However, Death had decided that enough was enough. For millennia, he'd been busting his ass for low wages, and not one "thank you" from his employer. In the end, who was

God to tell him how to do his job. If he thought about it, and he did very often, he'd never seen God lift a finger for anything he'd ever gotten. Everything always came easy to him. So, if Death, the being which billions upon billions of men and women fear wanted to take a load off his feet, by God he was going to take a load off his feet. So, for this reason, an no other conceivable reason, Death was not about to let himself get bullied off of a chair by a third-rate ghost who was incapable of crossing over on his own.

"To answer your question," he said, bringing his attention back to Fran, who was on the brink of having forgotten what she'd even asked in the first place. She gave him a death stare couple with hints of confusion, to which Death responded with an involuntary gulp out of fear. "Do you want the short or long answer?"

"Indulge me with the long one."

"That's what she said!"

Fran crossed her arms. Death looked around the room. He lifted his palms toward her as if he were saying *what? I thought it was funny.* To his dismay, Fran was not amused. Not even a little bit.

"Okay, fine. The truth is, souls," he pondered, repeating the word souls a few more times. At this moment, he wondered where he'd left his handbook which could have come in handy in a situation such as this one. It explained just about everything a reaper needed to know about reaping, and the benefit, use, average cost, and profit loss ratio. As he always did in class before assuming his role as Death, he had only ever glanced at the bright orange booklet adorned with only *So you're a reaper* on the soft cover. "I have no clue what a soul is for," he placed a thoughtful hand on his chin. Fran was without words. She stood up with the explicit intent of punching him in the face but kept herself from resorting to violence. Instead, she grabbed Death's chalice and took a swig. Death made his best attempt at stopping her, but she was speedy, almost disturbingly so.

Fran smacked her lips together as though she were attempting to concentrate on the flavor. It was a habit she picked up as a child after watching Bugs Bunny smack his lips together while eating his carrots. What began as an innocent imitation turned into a habit that caused anyone around her shoot dirty glances at her for her apparent lack of manners. "Yum, what's in this? Also, why is my soul worth so much? I'm a flaming bisexual atheist who is pro-choice." She flipped the chalice upside down and examined it for any last drops.

"Yes Fran, you can have the last bit of my delicious drink." He questioned why he'd ever choose to keep her around. "That could have killed you. You're lucky I wasn't day drinking. Have you ever had fresh battery acid? Because that could have been battery acid."

Fran shrugged. She ran her finger along the inside of his shiny cup and licked it, hoping for any leftover drink particles.

"It's strawberry acai. I like to be a fun guy, so I added some artificial flavoring. My buddy Natty D hooked me up with it."

"Natty D?"

"Natural disaster. Anyway, that guy hooked me up with some sudden gore he'd gotten after he unleashed an earthquake on the other side of the world. I had to help him collect millions of deaths. He collected the gore, while I was busy opening doors. It never occurred to me that gore would be such a good combination. I add a small block of dry Ice for effect." He then remembered he was angry at her for taking up the last of his drink. "If you weren't you, I would have reaped you early for that. Also, unlike for me, God likes you for some reason," he dematerialized the golden cup from Fran's hands.

"Heyy!" She traded the desk's surface for the more comfortable cushion her bed offered. "I would have never thought he was cool with me," she said.

"I don't understand it either. I barely tolerate you. Also, he sees what atheists all are about. You know what they bring to the table. Most of your lot, despite being little pricks, and your need to outwardly express your feelings against God and religion, are generally good people. I'm not so sure that you are, but that's not my call to make. I don't think he made a good decision with you."

"That's not what the price of my soul says. To me it sounds like I'm the best person." She gloated.

"What good is that to you now? You gave yours away for some un-godly reason."

"Like a dumbass," she smacked her forehead with her palm. "I would have sold the damn thing and gotten myself a much better apartment."

"Not a house?"

"Nah. Too much maintenance. Besides, I don't want to hire people to get things fixed. That, and I'm not ready for the commitment."

"Your ex-boyfriend being the victim of your latest clash with commitment is a great example of that." Fran grabbed a large pillow and placed it on her lap. She used it as an emotional support squish cushion. "Seriously. You flushed four years down the drain because he likes butt stuff? You know they make things to make stuff slippery."

"On that note," Fran brushed him off. She looked at her watch and realized she'd spent the better part of her day bickering with Death. Her heart stopped for a brief moment because she thought she had missed her morning shift at Starbucks. Then she realized she had the next two days off. That's not how she imagined her day going, though.

"Let me fill you in on a little secret," Death said. He leaned forward, being very careful not to give the chair ghost any opportunity to reclaim his chair. He was now at war, albeit a petty one, with the chair ghost. He was not about to lose. Especially now that he was ticked off for the lack of beverage that was once in his heavy golden cup. "You'd be fucked whether you gave your soul away as an act of kindness, or if you sold it for greedy purposes. You'd be so fucked, even if you lived the rest of your life being the epitome of saintly. The rest of your eternity would suck big ole hair balls. Big ones."

"I'm not sure that I care." Fran didn't care.

"Yeah, you will. With soul, you go to heaven."

"So that's a real thing? who'da thunk," her lips frowned in a not so upset way.

"Yeah, some religions got that part right. Although it's not exactly the way they say it is. It's not all butterflies and rainbows."

"What happens without soul?" She mockingly made a caveman sound as the words left her lips.

"You go to hell?" Death said very matter of fact like. It was the dumbest question he had ever heard, next to the question of lubricating an enema or not. He only wondered about them for the sake of one of his friends. Certainly not because he had ever, or would ever, think of inserting an enema up his boney behind.

"What's so bad about hell?"

"For starters, you constantly feel like you have to pee, but you can't. It doesn't matter how much you try, you can never squeeze even a drop out. It's sort of like having a bladder infection, or an enlarged prostate, but without all the other symptoms."

"That sounds awful," Fran placed her hand over where she thought her bladder rested.

"That's just the beginning. The Devil is kind of a douche, and severely sadistic. He doesn't allow any form of texting. Instead, he forces everyone to take a call, regardless of who is calling. He especially likes it when the person's mom calls. I don't know about you, but I hate answering my mom's calls. She's always asking me when I'm going to decide to get married. Damnit mom. I have to find someone first before I ever even think about getting married," Death shivered.

Fran's body shot violently and involuntarily in shear fear. "Please, I don't want to hear any more of this." She felt a wave of nausea and dread at the mere thought of having to actually answer her phone have a real, full length, thoughtful conversation with her mother. One with audible words, and structured sentences, and real time reactions. The idea of not having even a split second to fake a good *lol* was enough to induce a sudden cold sweat, which later would translate into nightmares beyond the level of comprehension the likes of which was literally unfathomable. She quickly reached for her trash can (thankfully she had remembered to switch out the liner that morning) and wretched into it. The entire contents of Death's beverage filled the trash receptacle. Death resented her for having wasted his liquidity treat in such a way.

"The bastard is so evil. He makes you follow through with plans you make that you never fully intend to keep."

Fran curled up into a ball onto her frigid wooden floor. She reached for a stuffed lamb under her bed she'd gotten at a thrift store that had been collecting dust for at least a month, or two. "So that's where you went." She gave the lamb a tight squeeze. "What a monster!" She continued after a sweet moment with her emotional support stuffed lamb.

"Hey," that's not my style. I'm just telling you what Lucy is into." Death conceded his chair to the ghost due to a need to stretch out his legs. His right butt cheek was beginning to feel numb, so he wanted to be proactive before it went any further. "Take that up with the big guy. I'm just here to fuck with people and be God's muscle."

Fran grunted from the floor. "What muscle?" she squeezed her lamb harder. A squeaky sound emanated from it, which startled her. She tossed it back under the bed, then noticed how hard the floor was and did nothing to improve her comfort.

Death paced back and forth in an attempt to regain feeling on his leg. He considered going back to his chair, but decided he hadn't the energy, nor the fucks, to force his will upon the chair ghost and regain his rightful place upon the chair. He did, however, tell him that he wouldn't be forgetting the ghost's unwillingness to give up the old dusty throne. The ghost simply mocked Death and pretended to be scared of the most likely empty threat.

"For your information," Death said after a brief nonverbal skuttle with the ghost. "I happen to be considered quite ripped within my species." *Come to think of it, do I have a species? I've never seen anyone else like me,* he thought. Fran rolled her eyes. He fought an almost compulsive urge to show her pictures of himself from back during the early days, around the beginning of time, in which he had a boney six pack. Back when he had first discovered the benefits of calisthenics. "There is one way you can benefit from your soul without selling it, or giving it away, though," he pondered. Death squinted his eyes as if to be deep in thought.

"I didn't think a stupid soul was freaking real!" She said. If she were standing, she would have stomped in jest, but instead settled for reaching back for her lamb and throwing it at Death's face. It his hard and forced his head back a little before it fell on the floor. He considered throwing something right back at her, but ultimately decided to pretend as though nothing had happened. Instead, he took a long, deep breath. For a brief moment, he considered not telling her how to make the best of her soul.

"You can, and, by technicality, are allowed to use your soul as collateral to secure a loan," he explained. Fran raised an eyebrow.

"I don't think I understand," she said with one low pitched grunt, then pushed herself up to a seated position, criss cross apple sauce style.

"When God wrote up the paperwork for the proper uses of any given individual's soul, he never mentioned anything about prohibiting anyone from putting up their souls as collateral. He simply states, "He, or she, who expires on earth and fails to produce the soul with which it left and bestowed upon at birth will be bound for eternity to the confines, rules and regulations, and management staff under the jurisdiction of Hell. Per statute 69-420b No soul no paradise clause.""'"

Fran ate up his every word the way a child does when their teacher reads a story to her class. Death materialized an ancient looking scroll, presumably the contract one signs shortly before being conceived. No one was allowed conception without signing the paperwork first. He read off the remainder of the clause because he hadn't quite committed the verbiage to memory.

"At which point, the Devil, ruler of Hell, shall claim ownership of the sad empty vessel, brittle shell of a person in perpetuity, and for the remainder of time. Should the empty shell outlive the vastness of time," Death paused. He took a breath and fixed a non-existent set of eyeglasses over the bridge of his nose. "His, or her, sentence will be automatically extended for no less than two additional time cycles without the possibility of parole." Death grinned at Fran. You fucked up, big time," he told her.

Fran experienced a short existential crisis. It was as though a shrewd of black clouds hovered above her head and were about to unleash an imminent thunderstorm. The very notion of having to talk to her mother over the phone was unimaginably horrifying enough to send her into a crushing depression, and severe bout of anxiety capable of inducing the worst of disabling oral canker sores the likes of which have no cure. She refused to accept her new fate. Her face hardened, seemingly in deep thought. Death paced from one end of the room to another. He was very intent on something. Finally, he landed directly in front of her paint chipped, pinewood dresser. Death took one finger and slid it across the surface, around the clutter of clothes and hair care products. It also served as a platform for a large, weathered mirror which donned several irregularly shaped dark spots that cast no reflections. He paused to look at a blemish beginning to surface at the base of his jaw. It was more of a jagged boney formation, almost like a calcified tumor than a typical blemish, but to him it was essentially the same thing. Death's species wasn't immune to the nuisances that humans experienced. Their issues just appeared in different ways. He leaned closer to the mirror and lifted his hands in preparation to pop the blemish like one does with zits. Once the blemish was popped, and its remnants slowly slid down the glassy surface, he took a moment to rummage through the two top drawers. The first one contained an assortment of brightly colored underpants. Not surprisingly, they were pretty small as they had to fit snuggly against Fran's petite frame. What threw him off was the fact that, not only were her undergarments unexpectedly colorful, they all had some sort of anime, or cartoon character print. He never took her to be the type to watch Naruto, or sailor moon, much less did he expect her to be a fan of Sponge Bob. This knowledge had only come to light as a result of him reaching for a pair of bright yellow undies with Sponge Bob's face on it. His nose was nearest the crotch. But, he supposed, having print in the form of her favorite reality T.V stars on her underwear would have been a bit more embarrassing.

Meanwhile, Fran slowly became reanimated. Her facial features regained the softness, yet exceedingly stern and stubborn qualities, it once had. She squinted at Death. He giggled, unaware that Fran had escaped her deep, depressing train of thought.

"What are you doing?" her angry voice sliced through his ear drums, causing him to jolt in fear. Death's nervous system glitched. He looked both ways as if trying to figure out where the angry voice came from, then dropped the yellow, child cartoon underwear on the floor. He slammed the drawer shut with one hand, while forgetting to remove the other and crushing his long boney fingers. The force from shutting the drawer severed all of his deathly digits, excluding his thumb. He quickly turned to address Fran. "You're back!" he clapped his mutilated hand against the good one. Then he quickly whipped his arms behind him the way a child does when he's concealing a delicious piece of candy. Fran's face dripped with bemusement. With his hand behind his back, still facing Fran, he discreetly cracked open the drawer and loudly whisper ordered his fingers to assume their original anatomical positions.

"I don't even want to know why," she was unable to finish her sentence. Instead, her arms dropped in disappointment in the type of company she chooses to surround herself with. She shrugged the painfully awkward interaction off. "I can get it back," she followed.

"Your underwear?

"Huh?"

"Nothing. You were talking about your soul, I knew that." Death looked at the underwear he'd thrown on the floor. He carefully scooted it under the dresser with one robed foot. "It took you this long to decide to get it back?"

"Yes, well, no. I don't know," she stood up. Fran walked towards Death and picked up the underwear from under the dresser. She glared at him, making Death flinch as he braced for the glare to become a well-placed punch to the gut. In this case, she was just happy that someone like her was capable of making something like a celestial being, the bringer of death, flinch like a little girl. She flung her underwear in circles with her index finger, a little too close to Death. He gained a sudden look of disgust, and shuffled away from her, but not without catching a full whip to the face from the yellow fabric. "I can just go back to the Asian market, find the guy, and ask for my soul back," she said while trying to contain her laughter after her underwear caught Death's exposed face.

Death cringed. He rubbed his face as though he were trying to remove a toxic substance off of it. "Do you even remember what the guy looks like?" The tone in his voice reflected the lack of confidence in her ability to find her soul and get it back. *There's no way in hell you're going to get that back,* he thought. Even the ghost held some reservations about her retrieving her soul. She balled her underwear up as small as they'd go and threw them onto the old chair. To her, this triggered the chair to violently fall, backrest to the floor, unexplainably. All

Death could see is the ghost getting hit on the face, pushing himself backwards as hard as he could in an effort to avoid, but fail, to get hit by such underwear, and falling backwards. The ghost's legs remained in the air for a brief moment. Death became giddy with glee at the site of his foe succumbing from the likes of Fran's butt huggers. He briefly considered helping the fallen soul onto his feet but decided to watch him struggle instead. "I don't think Tim appreciates your panties on his face," Death pointed to the fallen chair. The lights in her room flickered. "You may have pissed him off."

"He will get over it," Fran said. "The guy was short and stubby."

"Tim's actually kind of a hunk. He must have been a CrossFit guy, or maybe really into static exercises. He's about, ehh, six-foot-five?" Death clarified. His hands extended to about the height of Tim's stature.

"Not him," Fran playfully smacked Death's arm. He still winced. He never knew whether she was going to break him, or casually give him a friendly nudge. Regardless, a boney rattle escaped from within his robe. The structural integrity of his skeleton was no longer what it used to be. He was reminded of that little fact every time he found himself walking no further than a few feet. The noises had become so obvious to Fran that she'd been suspecting him of being creaky and rattle-y, but he'd play it off and say he was breaking in a new pair of shoes. "The guy at the Asian market, you dud. He's short and stubby. He's got a big pot belly and has an exaggerated Boston accent." Fran gestured a big, distended belly with her hands. Her back was arched in a way that made her stomach push forward. "His belly was this big." Her arms were rounded as far out as they could go. Her fingers didn't touch. Death walked back to the chair. He leaned forward and tilted it back to normal. He briefly considered taking a seat, but he bared no pleasure in claiming something no one else wanted. Instead, he walked up to her frosted window and looked out stoically. The temperature outside was actually much warmer than it was in her room, but he found himself scraping off some of the ice off the window to take a better look outside. Due to his incessant need to make his surroundings colder than a cadaver, he'd effectively made a freezer out of Fran's room. Luckily, this wasn't the first time he had loitered within Fran's room while he neglected to perform the duties his job required of him. She remained comfortable because of her wardrobe choice, despite his choice in room temperature. At this point, she had no choice but to tolerate him anyway. It wasn't like he was going to give up on forcing her to be afraid of him. So, she chose to deal with him instead. The best she could do was find better ways to tolerate him. If that meant that her closet now had to have more winter clothes, then that was just something she had to do.

"Fine, I'll come with!" He sounded excited.

"Don't you have work to do? Also, I didn't invite you. I don't know what this whole we things you're talking about is." She crossed her arms and raised an eyebrow at him.

"It's called automation. I have a guy that's taking care of it."

"Damn. AI is really stealing people's jobs."

Permits.

Chapter 4:

"The sushi was to die for. No pun intended," Fran glanced at her rearview mirror before switching lanes.

"Why no pun in- Ahh. I get it." Death looked over further to the right. "Careful! this guy is in your blind spot, and you do not want your insurance premium to go up." An obnoxious beeping sound from inside the cabin pierced through both of their ears, indicating that the passenger was not wearing a seatbelt.

"Stop being a back seat driver," she jerked her car back into her lane, narrowly avoiding merging into an unassuming minivan. Its driver laid his entire weight against the minivan's horn and flipped her off as he drove past her. Fran and Death yelled their share of profanities. That was until they noticed two children in the back of the minivan that were also flipping her off. They turned their face away from the angry driver and his equally angry children in an effort to prevent themselves from scarring the kids through an acute attack of road rage.

"What are you turning away for? They can't even see you," she now switched lanes successfully. She could see the angry man's squinty eyes dart at her from his rearview mirror. The kids on his back seat unbuckled their seatbelts and plastered their little faces against the rear window in efforts to deter Fran from getting any closer. One of the kids, a girl of about eight, licked the window while her younger brother pressed his nose against the glass.

Death's face looked disgusted. "Up until I met you, I had no clue that anyone else could see me." He stuck his split tongue out at the kids. Fran shook her head as if to tell them sorry for his behavior. "Who's to say this asshat, and his little asshats can't see me too?" From now on, my SOP"

Fran interrupted, "your what?"

"Standard operating procedure. Please, educate yourself lady. Anyway, my SOP is to act as though everyone could see me so as to not be caught wondering whether or not it's my job to claim animal souls. By animal souls I mean even souls I don't like. Like racists, and pedophiles."

"And? "She slammed on the brakes. "Sorry, it turned red." Death's head shot straight onto the dashboard. *Sorry!* She pantomimed.

"Oww!" he said. Death's arms clumsily searched for his head. "Over here. No, here!" he directed his arms. Fran reached over to the dashboard and helped him place his head back over his shoulders out of guilt. "Thanks. What do you mean and?" He couldn't tell if she was asking sarcastically, or if she genuinely wanted to know the answer. Erring on the side of caution, he chose to believe she wasn't being a brat for once. He feared he may regret that decision shortly though.

"Oh, I have no earthly clue," she said. Death turned to her. Cracking sounds crunched throughout the car louder than the music that played from her radio. Fran leaned her head back and laughed a loud, single laugh before pressing her foot on the gas.

"The light was still red," Death pointed out.

"Oh shit!" She looked around the way one does when they know they've fucked up. "No cop, no stop, bitches!" she said.

"And that's how you earn yourself a quicker visit with me," Death huffed. He crossed his arms. His head was still re-adjusting from the abrupt stop.

"What are you going to do about it?" she said. Her hands were ten and two on the steering wheel, like a bon-a-fide grandma's.

"I'm no snitch," Death said in his most gangster voice.

"I mean about the whole animal kingdom thing," she fought the urge to call him names.

"To tell you the truth, his voice was now no louder than a whisper. He looked like a kid who was trying to keep the fact that he had a candy in his pocket from his parents. Really, it was more like a whimper, but he wasn't about to call it that. Death leaned, slowly, closer to Fran. Just enough for him to feel the warmth from her pale cheeks emanate onto him. "I'm terrified to ask," his voice was now a fearful, high pitch squeal.

"So, you choose to ignore the problem?" she asked, very, very loudly. Death nodded in agreement. "What you're telling me, you're too chicken shit to ask God about your job description, and ignore the billions upon billions of unclaimed souls that now have to roam about the surface of the earth for the rest of eternity because you're too scared to own up to your mistakes?" An evil grin formed on her seemingly innocent looking face. She was truly deceiving that way. Death withered in pain as he half expected to be smitten by God at any moment now. He curled up into a ball, using his hood to cover himself even more. He took a quick glance at his notepad to see if he could claim Fran from the confines of her earthly body. Unfortunately, according to his notes, she was scheduled to die at a hundred and thirteen years of age, and that's if she wasn't careful about taking care of herself. The other number that indicated the oldest possibility was simply a question mark. This information being intel she was never to be privy of. Also, he was disappointed that he couldn't just take her now for being annoying.

"Since I can't claim you yet," he scowled, "I'm going to let that go for now."

Fran activated her blinker and turned left. She could see the smog clouds coming off of the industrial district in the distance. According to her GPS, they still had some time to go before reaching their Asian market destination.

"You want to get some sushi when we get there?" Kim and Ho are not only gods within the sushi community, they are a really sweet old couple that managed to break out of North Korea." Fran spoke as she avoided massive potholes on the road. Some had been recently fixed by messy patches of gravel. Others were deep enough to fuck up a small car's chassis (such as the one Fran was driving), so she made sure to drive carefully around them. Her biggest concern was being pulled over by the cops on account of all the swerving. Surely, though, the cops around that area must have been understanding based upon the size of the car fucking up holes on the ground.

"You're driving like a mad man. Woman. Is that phrase interchangeable? I don't know anymore. Also, Eww. Kim Jung Un," Death shivered. "You know, I've done a lot of work up in North Korea. There's nothing, and I mean NOTHING, to do up in that bitch," he said. He tried to shake off the memories of being bored in one of their abandoned super massive buildings.

"That's what Kim and Ho said," Fran said. She tilted her head upwards in a way that indicated that her eyesight was going to shit, and she was having trouble keeping up with the potholes. As much as she tried not to, she managed to drive straight over a few that really didn't cause too much damage to her car. However, she apologized to her little vehicle every time she hit a hole.

"Really?" Death asked, almost happy that someone else felt the same way about the hermit nation.

"No, you insensitive jackass," she scolded him. They are an oppressed nation, living under the rule of one of the worst dictators the world has ever seen. They weren't trying to casually find something to do on a Friday night and get their freak on."

"You think he's an evil dictator? Before being assigned to earth, you know, before the existence of humans, I had a gig on the outskirts of the Milky Way, on a planet called pluton Major. Tiny little, toxic green colored planet orbiting a dying star. It wasn't toxic, just full of really dark green fauna that gave it an eerie appearance. Their technological advances would make earth seem like child's play if it were still around. Anyway, the entire planet was ruled by one lanky little dictator called Eek Nom Vator, or something like that. I could never quite grasp their dialect. I learned their language after about a hundred years of being there, but I couldn't roll my *R*s the way they did. Eeek, that guy, was a real dictator." Fran smacked his shoulder. He attempted to block her hand but wasn't fast enough. She had ninja like speed and precision.

"Really?" She looked at him incredulously. The fact that there was life on a different part of the galaxy, and not just in her small blue planet, went completely unrecognized. She was more in awe at how Death was admiring someone like Jung Un.

"Tragically, their entire civilization destroyed themselves during a nuclear civil war while trying to strip Eek from his power. There was the west side, Eeek sympathizers, and the east side. Don't ask me how they divided up one side from the other. That guy, though. He was one of the best dictators in the history of the universe. It took me months to collect all those souls. I'm talking about trillions of souls. Yeah, the planet was a little overpopulated, considering how small the planet was. I think the war was more about resources than having Eek kicked out of office. He was hoarding the last bit of potable water and would only distribute it to those who were loyal to him. Those who weren't were left to die of thirst and starvation. The situation got so bad that near the end of their existence they began to eat one another. It was preferable to eat those on opposing sides of the war, but they weren't past eating one of their own in extreme cases. It was really, really brutal. I was the only one collecting those souls. No one was thinking about me when they decided to kill each other. How inconsiderate of them. I still have PTSD from having to work seven days a week for months on end."

Fran's eye twitched. She was normally never speechless. However, she often chose not to speak because she hated everyone around them, but this was different.

"Then I came here," he said giddily. "It was a relief, too, because I was aching for a break. When I got here there were fewer than a million of your hair, knuckle dragging ancestors, so it was a breeze. Most of you died from being eaten, or eating barriers, or a simple cold." Fran kept her eyes on the road as she avoided a rough patch of concrete. She patted her car as Death continued. "Ya'll were so dumb. If you asked me, you guys aren't so different now than how you were then. There's just a lot less hair. Most of you are still pretty dumb though." He looked at Fran. "What do you intend to do once we get to your friend Frank's place?"

Fran's eyes were glazed over. Death had witnessed this several times before. She had spaced out. He waved his hand in front of her eyes, then she took a long, deep breath.

"There she is!" he shouted.

"Huh? Who, umm. I'm going to walk in there, and ask him very nicely?"

"Good luck with that."

Fran's face failed to conceal her feelings of self-doubt. "He seemed like a pretty nice guy. I'm sure he's also very reasonable." Death's head twitched. It was like he'd gotten a cold chill, but it came off more as him having lost any faith in her. "What?" she asked.

Death started wildly sniffing the air around him. Fran discreetly leaned over to smell her armpits as she approached a stop sign. Her upbringing forced her to lock her doors as a panhandler approached the side of her car, which gave her a dreadful guilty feeling for having done so. Deciding she was being classist, and maybe a touch racist, she rolled her window down. The man beside her had a patchy head of short, curly hair, and was very clearly black. Well, more mocha. His ethnicity was a little ambiguous, but he was certainly a minority of some sort. His clothes appeared as though they'd been a few years old, and maybe his only set. There were holes, and crusted patches of dirt all around it. Fran reached into her cupholder where she would regularly toss loose change after buying fast food on days she was too tired, or too lazy, to cook for herself at home. She grabbed the change, a few quarters that came out to about three dollars for seventeen scents and reach out her window to hand the poor man her change. The man grabbed her hand and started yelling incoherently. His mouth lacked most of his front teeth, and she could smell a putrid odor coming from him, along with a strong whiff of alcohol, which was probably what Death had been sniffing out moments ago. Fran yelled with the man, and so did Death. until he let go of her hand. The change remained in her clench fist. They yelled at one another's faces for approximately thirty seconds before pressing her foot down on the gas pedal as far as it went. Her tires spun, causing the old man to jump back so as to not have his toes run over. A thick cloud of white burning rubber trailed the wheels as her car gained enough traction to move forward. The man behind them was left engulfed within the white toxic cloud.

"My spider senses are tingling, quick! Turn right here!" Fran did as he said. The adrenaline rush rushing through her veins forced her to act without thinking. She was now in survival mode and was not about to let the homeless man catch up to them. She imagined him running behind them like the liquid metal cop did in Terminator. Her heart raced. Her hands shook, but they remained gripped tightly at ten and two. Despite the distress, the year in driving school she had to endure in high school stuck to her enough to keep her hands at the grandma position. "Left! Now! Left!" Death shouted. He looked intent. She'd never seen him this serious, so she did as he said again. Her car drifted, Tokyo Drift style, as they turned. She screamed. He screamed as well while holding on to the handle above him. Fran had no handle to grasp, so she white knuckled the steering wheel, which would later create a permanent indent on it. Her lungs fought for air. She gulped for any bit of oxygen. "Stop!" Death shouted. Fran pressed on the brakes. The car slid about fifteen feet before coming to a full stop. Tire marks trailed behind them from where she initially engaged her brakes. Her hair had become messy from the action. Sweat poured from her forehead. The areas on her shirt below her armpits were now a darker shade of black as it absorbed a rush of sweat.

"What?" She looked at him, still struggling to catch her breath.

"Burger King!" He pointed to her left. She turned her head slowly. Her clear window revealed the restaurant. Some people walked in and out. There was a line of cars waiting anxiously at the drive through line.

"I'm going to kill you," she said. Before he could open the door, Fran pressed on the gas and drove away. Death *awed* in disappointment. She followed the new recalculated directions her GPS suggested. Death's mouth watered for a juicy burger with jalapenos. He whimpered once he realized Fran wasn't going to turn around and wait in the drive-through line. "The sun is going down. We have less than ten minutes before we get there, and I do not!" She looks him dead in the eye as she reaches forty miles an hour. She's unblinking. Death shifts nervously in his seat as if to say he feels uncomfortable with her taking her eyes off the road. He finally chooses to put his seat belt to good use. "I don't intend on missing out on delicious sushi because you got a craving for burgers!" her hair fell onto her face. She attempted to blow it away from her eyes with her mouth a few times before redirecting her attention to the road ahead of them. Death's heart rate returned to normal once her focus returned to where it should have been. He considered making a snarky joke but decided against it for fear of getting into a head on collision. He'd recently run out of paid sick days, so he wasn't about to have to spend a long span of time at home without getting paid.

The rest of the car ride was silent, minus the purr of Fran's hybrid engine, and the gentle hum of her tires rotating against the sparse patches of pothole-less asphalt. Death reached toward her radio, but Fran slapped his boney hand away. He took the hint. Quietly, he sat like a kid does after witnessing his normally patient mother lose her shit after he'd pissed in the bathtub for the hundredth time and being told to cut that shit out every single time, uncertain for his future, but a hundred percent sure that regardless of what he said next within the next thirty minutes, the next words coming out of his mouth would accompany him by his death certificate. Death twiddled his thumbs. He cleared his throat once, which he instantly regretted as Fran shot him a stare that would knock the soul out of any normal mortal. He looked away from her in sheer fear. He'd never seen her so flustered. Truly, such a small woman was not one to be messed with. Not even Death dared pushing her any further. For a moment, he worried that God would discover her talents and replace him altogether. Then he thought the thought was nonsense, or at least he hoped. He was now full of doubt. He knew he didn't have any marketable skills, outside of being Death, so he wasn't sure what he'd do to make a living if God decided to replace him with Fran. Surely, he could give retail a try, but then remembered he hated people as much as Fran did. Fuck, if she could do it, so could him, but where would he start? It's not like he had any interaction with a human aside from the brief moments he'd speak to them while ushering them into the afterlife. Fran herself was no one to learn from either. He'd witnessed her crossing the street, and walking well out of her way with the sole purpose of avoiding someone she thought she'd known because she didn't want to say hi, and fake being interested in what the other person had going on. He did have a degree in criminology, so maybe he could put that to good use. He only had it because it was a pre-requisite to becoming Death. Well, at least before God decided that the best business plan involved a healthy dose of nepotism. Ultimately, Death shook the feeling off the way a dog does the post bath shake onto its owner's clean furniture. God would never replace him, and that's what he was going with, for his own sake.

"That's odd," she said. Her rage now subsided. He was thankful to her for breaking the nail-biting silence. Death hesitated to ask a follow up question.

"What's odd?" he braced himself as he asked. He closed his eyes in anticipation of any degree of violence toward him and was relieved to learn he was in the clear after about a minute.

"I could have sworn this is where the Asian market was." She drove slowly near what should have been the pedestrian entrance to the market. Fran Parked her car across the street. Her confusion was now at an all-time high.

"Are you sure we are in the right place?" Death kicked an old milk crate as he walked near the old market entrance. There were piles of trash being gently pushed around by the wind around them. Pallets of discarded wood sat where the fish vendor's store used to sit. A homeless man used some of the wood planks as a makeshift bed. He covered himself with an old, raggedy, red sleeping bag. Rats ran around him as he slept, stealing any bit of food they could find, including munching on his clumpy hair.

"Should we make sure that guy is alive?" Fran asked.

"Nah, I'm sure he's okay," Death said. He walked up to the homeless man, and kicked the pallet on which he was sleeping. The homeless man made a snoring sound. "See?"

"I think this is the right place," she answered Death's question. Fran turned to Death. He was now facing a large orange sign. From the looks of it, he had the body language of someone who was struggling to read.

"Are you going blind? Or do you not know how to read?" she asked as she walked past the sleeping homeless man. He smelled similar to the man they had encountered by the stop sign, only there was also a strong hint of urine and a puddle beside him proving that theory.

"I know how to read," Death said. "I just need to get my reading glasses, is all."

"Right," Fran said.

"I'm serious!" He said. The old homeless man turned toward the wall behind him, farting as he shifted in his sleeping bag. "Come to think of it, I think they are right here." Death fumbled a hand inside of his robe, and produced a pair of thin, wiry looking, round reading glasses. Fran was impressed at how stylish they made him look. It was borderline attractive. Then she wondered why he would need glasses if he didn't have eyes. Almost immediately after that, she shamed herself for even considering the possibility of Death being even remotely attractive. The thought brought on the idea that she needed more friends with less visible bones, and maybe some skin, or even a heartbeat. Maybe someone her own age would be healthy. All the people her age annoyed her though. They were either getting married, and starting a wonderful life, with many equally happy friends, or they were on their second wife, getting ready to have their first kid (whether they planned one or not), and settling down way before they were ready. She was sort of an anomaly in that she didn't care to be in a relationship, or have kids, or friends, or interact with other people. Her priorities were more on par with getting out of poverty, and maybe finding an apartment, possibly even a condo, with thicker walls so that she didn't have to hear her neighbors do it every night. For one, she was overdue for a fire-y night of passion with a hot piece of meat. She didn't care if it was a guy or a girl, but some level of human touch would have been nice, and her neighbors were really good at reminding her that she was going to die alone. So, even she wanted to settle down, and have a bunch of oops kids, she would need to find a partner for that first. She'd also have to crawl out of poverty. She was not about to bring a kid into the world knowing that she was destitute herself. So, she guess that maybe being alone was a good thing. She just needed to spend less time with Death for fear of becoming more of a freak.

Death stared at her as she struggled internally. This was normal for her, but now she'd been in deep thought for longer than usual. He was beginning to worry she may not get out of it. This was different from when they were in the car, and he waved his hand in front of her. She was there, but not there. Unlike when she spaces out and isn't there. Her face twisted in odd ways. Sometimes she looked disgusted, others she looked genuinely concerned. He couldn't quite understand what she was going through. He'd come to realize that her concerned face was oddly like that of her thinking face. It was always a spectacle to be seen. If it weren't for the lousy storage space on his phone, he'd taken a video of her and used it to blackmail her later. Having the phone numbers of all the celestial required a great amount of memory, though. He couldn't risk corrupting it over a video of a woman's face malfunctioning. Also, he was only carrying his company cell phone. He'd left his personal phone in his other robe at home, and he doubted he had enough time to open a wormhole, walk through its threshold, toss the dirty robes, look through each of their pockets in search of his phone, and come back before she came to. He licked his finger, getting it as wet and slobbery as he could, and aimed for her ear. He quickly put his slobbery finger away as she rejoined him.

Death redirected his attention back to the orange sign. His glasses sat snuggly against his face. Fran wasn't sure how he managed to keep them up, considering he had no nose on which to sit his glasses, or ear to help hold them up. "Looks like whatever was here got shut down by the city!" he shouted. Fran winced and turned away from him as he was basically screaming directly into her ear.

"I see that now, but why?" She asked.

"You're still reading that?" Death asked smugly.

"Shut up, I'm a slow reader." Fran stood on her tiptoes as she inspected the rest of the sign for further signs as to why the market was shut down. Death briefly considered helping her by picking her up, then remembered the last time he made her feel short. She was attempting to reach the top shelf of her cupboard, so he reached over her to grab a cup for her. She'd ripped off the limb with which he helped because he had insinuated she was short by helping her. The memory still haunted him. So, he let her calves burn while she stood on her tiptoes.

"Are you freaking serious!" She yelled while placing her hands above her head. She paced back and forth in distress. "A permit!?" she repeated angrily.

"Looks like several by the lack of any street vendors, according to how you described the place." Death went on. "So, this means no sushi. I hope you weren't hungry. We could have gotten something back at Burger King. If we hurry, we could probably get there before the crackheads start looking through their trash," he continued. His mouth watered for their fries, and their frozen chocolaty cheesecake. Then he remembered he was broke.

Fran took off running abruptly, deeper into the abandoned alley as he was getting ready to ask her to buy him dinner. He followed, but only because he feared that she was running away from something he was yet to be aware of, and he didn't want to be a substitute for whatever was chasing her. It didn't occur to him that she may have been upset at the fact that every single one of the street shops had been shut down, with prejudice, for not having the appropriate paperwork. A sheet of paper that indicated they were paying taxes for services rendered, or goods provided. Which explained why Fran then worried that the man who conned her out of her soul was no longer there. She dropped to her knees. Death approached her from behind, quietly. He was aware of what was at stake for her, and now she stood no chance of ever recovering her soul. Fran let out a heartfelt cry. Even though he was the God, and ruler of death, he was not beyond feeling empathetic towards those he cared about. A knot formed in the depths of his being. The image of his friend suffering, the strongest woman he'd ever come to know, sobbing so hopelessly broke whatever remnants of a heart he still had. He fought tears of his own in support of her. He placed a boney hand on her shoulder and gave it a gentle squeeze.

"It's going to be okay, friend," he said empathetically. Tears fell down her face uncontrollably. A single tear strolled down his.

She sniffled. Her head hung towards the pebbly concrete. Small rocks and pieces of old shattered glass pressed harshly against her knees, but not hard enough to break through the fabric of her pants. "No, it won't. Things will never be okay again." Her words were heavy, cutting deeply against the little humanity Death had in him. He gave her a moment out of respect. He couldn't imagine the feeling of knowing he'd lost his soul. Especially knowing he'd been the one to give it away in the first place. He did his best to understand how Fran was feeling.

"They had the best sushi!" Fran burst into a free flow of tears. She wailed like she'd never wailed before. She even looked up at the sky as tears ran down her face. Her black hair was even messier now than it had been when she drove away from the screaming homeless man at the stop sign. She let herself cry the ugliest of cries. Snot oozed from her nose. She used her sleeves to clean them up.

Death nodded sympathetic nod. His insides were in knots. "Wait, what?" the words she uttered lingered around in the air. His sympathy immediately escaped him.

"Oh hi, Catgatha!" Fran said in a happy, high pitch obnoxious squeak. She perked up instantly upon seeing the slow-moving cat. She rubbed up against Fran's thigh the way she had when Franks storefront was still up. All Death could think of doing was giving himself the biggest of face palms that he could imagine giving himself. His shoulder slumped, and he removed his hand from Fran's shoulder. At that precise moment, something in the air felt off, at least for Death. It was as though the air around them suddenly had become more viscous. He could taste a subtle hint of sulfur and despair floating about. Only a celestial with his experience and expertise would be able to pick up on it. He scanned their surroundings but failed to locate a visible entity. He took a discreet, but powerful defensive demeanor. Something wasn't right, and he could tell they were in imminent danger. At the very least, Fran's life now rested entirely upon his hands.

"Hi Richard," he heard from down below. It weaved in and out of Death's robe. The soft embrace of a cat's fur brushed up against his boney shins. "Not now," he said. His mind was too busy formulating a plan of attack in the event that he'd have to heroically fend off any attackers. He was close to figuring out what exactly was off about that place. However, he couldn't quite put his finger on it. Death kneeled to pet the cat who looked at him with a lazy gaze. He stood up and scratched his head.

"Who is Richard?" Fran asked Catgatha. The fact that she'd just heard a cat speak was yet to be registered.

"That's my name. Now hush. I'm trying to figure out where this weird feeling I'm getting is coming from." Death picked Catgatha up and started petting it.

Fran became worried. "Are we safe?" She looked around, and above her at the roof tops cautiously. Her instincts forced her to yank the cat away from Death so that she could cuddle with it nervously.

"We will be as long as you do exactly as I say," Death said. He put up his fists in a defensive stance. He'd never actually had to fight anyone, though. The way he stood looked more like he was bracing himself from a falling object. His arms covered the top of his head, and he hunched over the way someone does when they are walking under something that's too low to the ground. He walked in front of Fran, pushing her behind him in a heroic defensive stance.

"Richard, it's me!" Catgatha said from within Fran's tight embrace. She struggled to breathe as she pushed out a few words. Catgatha struggled her way out of Fran's death grip, and climbed up to her shoulders, wrapping herself like a scarf around Fran's neck. Fran winced in pain as she dealt with Catgatha's claws. Death shushed her as she made Fran yelp from her sharp claws.

"You guys know each other?" Fran said in between a few painful yelps. Death put up a finger as though demanding her to stop talking, but she continued. "More importantly, you have a name? I thought you were just Death," she asked.

Death glared at her for disregarding his orders. "Yes, now please. I'm securing the perimeter for your safety. Your life may be on the line, and I'm the only one who can protect you. If you keep interrupting me with stupid questions you can die at any moment," he said. Then it hit him. He stood still, taking a further moment to process the fact that a cat had just blurted his name without regard to his very well-known wish not to be called that. The only one who ever called him by his name was his mother, but he hadn't seen her in eons. There was only one other being who knew of his name, well, beside God. Death had to fill out his tax paperwork, and God, along with his accountants, had to see his legal name. The only other being, beside God, his accountants, and his mother, had been drafted by the devil back in early human history to fight the great war. That's a history lesson for another day. However, that being was Catgatha, Death's former pet.

Catgatha caught a glimpse of a rat the size of a small Pomeranian. "Excuse me. I'm famished, and I've now seen my next snack." Catgatha ran after the rat, which must have been at least thirty-five pounds, or more.

"I didn't know cats could talk," Fran said. She was surprisingly not shocked about her new discovery, or maybe she was so in shock that her brain went insane, and she fooled herself into thinking it was normal. After all, she was friends with Death, so perhaps, maybe, she wasn't going insane after all.

"Oh yeah. Funny enough," he explained. "Ninety percent of the cats on earth are capable of speech. They are generally a bunch of assholes, though.

"That explains so much," Fran stares off into the distance, watching Catgatha as she stalks her obese prey. Meanwhile, Catgatha shook her butt a few times before pouncing toward the gigantic dog size looking rat, and bit it with one enormous bite. It was truly a sight to be seen. She crunched down hard on the rat's fat bones and through its soft tissue. Her teeth pierced straight through the rat's aorta, causing a violent gush of blood to shed all over the abandoned alleyway, sending the rat hybrid into a quick and almost painless death. She then returned with a trophy in hand, or mouth. She coughed a long, thin vertebrae, and a wet and sticky clump of rat hair. It sounded as though she was choking as the excess fought to exit her body. Two seconds later, Death witnessed a rat Grim Reaper open up a portal next to the now blood covered cat. The soul of her recently eaten prey slid out of her mouth in the form of thick celestial smoke. The Rat Death then swung its scythe in the most effortless manner. He doesn't use it to slice the rat's soul, but more so as a tool to gently aid the recently deceased soul toward the right direction. Generally, a newly deceased being tends to be beyond disoriented, with the whole having just died thing. The job of the Grim Reaper is often severely misunderstood. Death never actually kills anybody, or thing, which is a rather annoying misconception. He, or she, is but a shepherd herding its stock back to a restful place. Rat Death exuded an air of professionalism and ancient wisdom to it. His focus was like nothing Fran's Death had ever seen, including within himself. Rat Death stopped his client just before entering his portal, and had him sign a series of legal documents, and addendums, and non-disclosure agreements, not to mention four newly added affidavits. He gracefully dematerialized the paperwork and welcomed the rat to the afterlife.

"She just happens to speak every conceivable language in the universe because she's a demon," Death says. Fran could tell he was bothered by the haste and efficiency with which the rat Death operated. Death was just relieved that he didn't have to sneak behind God's back and as HR about the inter species reaper policies. The guilt of potentially ignoring the souls of billions upon billions of souls over God knows how many millennia melted off of his shoulders. He looked up, happy that he didn't have to come clean.

"I always knew demons were real!" Fran said.

"Yet, you were an avid God denier?" He questioned her moral compass.

"It makes more sense." She stopped herself before ranting about religious nut jobs concealing their hatred toward anyone who doesn't share their same beliefs, and making themselves appear as though they are the most righteous God-fearing people.

Catgatha nodded. She rubbed herself against Fran. "What brings you back?" she asked.

Fran's thoughts derailed. "How come I've never heard a cat talk before?" She was skeptical.

Death pats his robe in search for his handbook. He'd been looking on the wrong side of his robe for nearly a million years now. It was in the pocket he never cared to check. Mostly because he had forgotten it even existed. He flips through it and finds the chapter that talks about the Rat Grim Reaper. His curiosity is peaked, so he checks for the existence of other species. He considers searching for unicorns but feels silly even wondering about the possibility of their existence. For good measure, and scientific purposes, he flips the pages until he finds a unicorn. "So, they are real!" he says out loud as he jumps in excitement. He consumes as much information from his handbook as possible.

"Don't mind him," Fran says. "So, how do you two know each other?" she asks. Petting her now felt different, considering the recent discovery of her sentience. Fran stood up and inspected the site where Frank's tent used to be.

"I used to be his pet before being drafted by the Devil," she said. "I still have some PTSD, so I'd rather not go too much into it. Let's just say, it's really hard for me to be around unicorns. I go into a murderous rage if I even think there may be one around me." Catgatha shivered subtly as memories of her slaughtering unicorns, and her near death experience as they held her as a prisoner of war. She had escaped near certain death as they slowly declawed her during one of their torture sessions. The unicorns were trying to extract information about her knowledge of certain weapons of mass destruction, and their whereabouts, but she managed to keep her lips shut even as they pulled her last claw and readied themselves to pluck each of her nine lives, one by one, by unimaginable methods. One being the playing of a song by Rebecca Black about Friday. They liked to play songs that were near stroke inducing on loop until the recipient of such torture either killed itself or suffered a massive stroke. In this instance, Catgatha had decided to hang herself from the rafters, causing her to lose one of her nine lives. When she came to, the unicorns had already devised yet another way they'd claim another one of her lives. The plan was to give Catgatha millions consecutive baths until she died of exhaustion and anxiety. Even though she was a demon, she shared the same hatred for water as her non demon cat species had. She was halfway into the million baths when the war ended, claiming the devil as the victor. If not for the victory, she was surely going to lose a second life closer to the seven hundred thousandth bath. Her heart could only take so much. She would never have made it to the millionth bath. Just thinking about her time in service had a tendency to cripple her, but the war was now far enough behind her that she was able to shake it off a little quicker. Fortunately, she had also learned how to repress those memories, so mentioning the fact that she had PTSD no longer triggered the excruciatingly painful memories.

Fran's eyes grew two times their normal size. She stood still, not really knowing what to tell a shell-shocked demon cat.

"What brings you back?" Catgatha asked.

Death absent mindedly walked away as he explored more of his handbook. The information in it was rather astounding.

"Frank. I came to get my soul back. What the hell happened here?" Fran asked. Catgatha licked her paws after having had such a hardy meal.

"The city came in and kicked everyone out, including Frank," she switched paws. Her movements were slow and intentional. The slowness was more so a result of her body struggling to process the dead body of a thirty-five-pound rat. There was a brilliant shine to her jet-black fur that showed she took very good care of her hygiene. She seemed out of place considering the fact that she was exceptionally well kept, but was surrounded by heaps of garbage bags, foul odors, rats bigger than Catgatha herself lurking just about everywhere and homeless people pissing against any garbage cans they could find.

"Long story," Catgatha's lazy gaze caught Fran's eyes. Her eyes were nearly hypnotizing. She spoke smoothly, almost as though her voice was meant to be a weapon meant to lure her prey. "The city got mad because Kim and Ho decided to put their foot down on a city official," Catgatha said.

Fran fought the urge to sit. The floor beneath her feet was stained with substances she doubted belonged to this earth. "Hell yeah, Kim and Ho!" Fran blurted. Her skinny arms flailed hi above her head from excitement.

"The Asian market had actually been here for years. The city was well aware that all of these guys were operating without a license or permits of any kind. And, even if the commercial alleyway residents wanted to be good, law-abiding citizens, the alley simply wasn't zoned for the circus it had become," Catgatha recounted. Fran squatted. Her feet were planted flatly, firm against the ground. She hugged her knees to gain her balance. She'd always been unnaturally flexible, so her resting stance posed zero stress against her joints.

"Did you guys know there are dragon reapers?" Death asked. His handbook occluded his face. There was an unidentifiable sticky object stuck to his shoe, causing him to struggle with every step as he paced. Fran's face lit up because that meant that she could go searching for one after talking to Catgatha. Death lifted a finger without looking at either of them. "But they're off planet, a few hundred light years away. Maybe I should schedule a little soiree with it and the unicorns." He licked his index finger and flipped a page. Fran looked at him with disappointment, defeated.

"Is he always this oblivious?" Catgatha asked. Fran nodded. "He wasn't that bad when I was his pet. Anyway, where was I?" She fought the urge to groom herself. Her head twitched as she fought the compulsion.

"Zoning," Fran said confidently.

"Ahh, that's right. Everyone knows Chicago is super corrupt, right?" Catgatha asked.

"Right," Fran said as though she actually knew. She was the worst person to ask about politics. For her, the whole government thing was just a way for old white guys to fuck with a population and get what they want. The closest she got to knowing anything about government was when she was in eighth grade, and her class was trying to nominate a class president. Even then, she had no clue what a class president could do or was capable of. However, she tended to blindly agree to anyone asking her a question, especially if she didn't know what they were talking about.

"Well, some city official was a huge, and I mean huge, fan of Kim and Ho. The sushi restaurant owners were entirely okay with letting the guy eat there for free as long as he pretended that all of their collective ducks were in order. However," Catgatha paused. She became distracted by the way her tail swayed almost as if it had a mind of its own. She stared at it for a moment the way she did before pouncing upon her prey and proceeded to claw at it. Catgatha rolled around on the dirty ground twice before grabbing a hold of her tail. The assault then triggered her hind legs to reflexively kick. Her face caught the sharp claws at the end of her fluffy little toes, and she meowed angrily at herself. Fran attempted to break up the fight, but she didn't know if her arm would come out of the scuffle unscathed, so she let the altercation take place until Catgatha's upper half of her body declared a decisive victory against her tail and her hind legs. She sat breathlessly before remembering that Fran was staring at her, waiting for her to finish explaining whatever it was that she was explaining. "Have you noticed that it's more expensive to buy the same number of groceries this year than ever before?" She continued as though she had not just beaten herself up.

Fran felt it better not to ask questions about what she'd just witnessed. Instead, she pictured her most recent bank statements. "Yeah," She began to wonder why it was costing her a hundred dollars for a couple of grocery bags worth of goods, when the same amount of money used to buy her a full shopping carts worth of food, and other miscellaneous items. She stretched her arm in front of her and counted her fingers. She scrunched her nose as if to calculate an unsolvable equation.

"Let me tell you, INFLATION!" Catgatha slowed her words for emphasis. Her body tensed so tightly that Fran could see her neck muscles stick out through her thick black fur coat. "Kim and Ho, being the excellent bookkeepers that they were, took a good look at their numbers, and noticed that, with the unregulated rising cost of food, feeding the city official pro-bono was cutting deeply into their profit margin. So, what did they do?"

Fran stared. She was hooked on every word that left Catgatha's lips. Catgatha looked back at her. Fran looked longer, wondering if the talking cat was expecting an answer, or if it was a rhetorical question. She had a habit of not understanding when people were actually asking her a question, or if she was expected to nod and listen. Death continued ranting on about his handbook, but it all sounded like gibberish. The rat Reaper helped another rat off in the distance. It hugged the soul rat before entering a heavenly portal, and right after having it sign all the legal documents one needed to sign. Fran tapped her fingers against her bent knees. They were beginning to ache from squatting for so long. She noticed that her pants were beginning to show signs of moderate signs of wear and tear. For a brief moment, she'd forgotten what her and Catgatha were talking about. She began to question why she wasn't more surprised that she was still talking to an alley cat in full, coherent sentences. She wasn't sure if she was suffering a stroke or not. Then she wondered if she'd kept her front door wide open, or if she'd closed it before leaving her house. It was an irking feeling, and it was starting to make her worry. Then she remembered that the cat had been drafted by devil himself to fight a war she had no business fighting in. From what she'd told Fran, Catgatha was rather fond of unicorns. Then the realization that the cat may be a war criminal dawned upon her and debated whether she'd be complicit of harboring a war criminal simply by talking to her. Fran looked at the Rat Reaper and couldn't help to compare it with her version of Death. Come to think of it, besides the one time he witnessed him taking her grandma, she'd never actually seen him do any kind of work. At least not what he'd been hired to do. She remembered the cat was probably still waiting for an answer. "They-"

"They broke things off with the guy, that's what," Catgatha interrupted. She seemed proud of having known this as if she placed value within herself based upon the amount of knowledge she kept in her brain. "The city official guy got pissed. He stormed out of the restaurant, and that was that. Right?"

Fran felt like she'd been set up for another game of is it a rhetorical question. "Right," she nodded.

"Wrong." Fran's face became visibly confused. She stood up because her knees began to hurt. "Like the chicken shit he was, he pleaded his case to the district attorney and secured a cease-and-desist letter for everyone here. Then, he ordered them to vacate the premise with the threat of a mountain of legal fees and their first-born children if they failed to comply."

"No one here had any permits?" Fran asked. She stretched her legs and fought a sure to be imminent Charlie horse. Her left thigh started to cramp, but she fought the urge to fall to the floor, in pain, so she punched it out of her. Then she attempted to walk the pain away discreetly. She walked on her heels as she kept her legs as straight as possible. Otherwise, the cramp on her thigh attacked her without prejudice. Death walked up behind her and used her as support as he leaned against her and showed her a picture of a bunny reaper.

"What do you think about this guy? He looks a little pretentious if you ask me," he told Fran. She ungracefully attempted to move away from him. The weight of his bones was too much for her cramped leg. He stumbled, but managed to regain his balance, as Fran moved away.

"Not one single person," Catgatha said in a near whisper. She turned her head from one side of the alleyway to the other as if to make sure that no one was listening to her. She was raised knowing that snitches get stitches, and she was no snitch. At the very least, she didn't want to appear as one. She was more than willing to participate in a good gossiping session.

"Not even Frak?"

"Especially him. That rat bastard," she said. Rat death overheard her say this from a long distance. He swung his scythe angrily at her, then entered his portal along with his client.

"Where is he now?" Fran asked. Her charlie horse was now subsiding.

"I don't know. We used to be roommates. I met him off of craigslist after the war, but I moved out and sort of started living in his tent, rent free. I hated waking up every morning to nail trimmings on the couch, or pubes on the toilet, so we made a deal. If I could live in his tent for free, I'd act as a demon security cat and eat whoever broke in. Unfortunately, no one ever broke in. I really hoped for someone to do so, though. It's been so long since I've eaten a human, and I really needed an excuse to eat gourmet human meat."

Death felt a vibration in one of his pockets. He ignored it. The information he was learning from the handbook made a lot of things he reserved doubts about were now being made clear. It made him regret having waited so long to actually take a look at it. The vibrations continued in his pocket until he remembered he was carrying a phone. The device was still a relatively new concept to him, considering the fact that he'd only had one for about twenty years. Compared to the near eternity he'd already been alive; it was difficult for him to remember that he was now connected to the outside world twenty-four hours a day. The vibrating from within his robe forced him to close his book. He grunted as he reached for his cell phone. His screen displayed a frantic text from God.

God: We've got a problem. Call me. Now!

Death: Can't. Busy.

God: No, you're not. You need to call me, so help me God.

Death: I'm in the middle of something. It's an important meeting. Lots of important VIPs

Death rolled his eyes at God's insipid texts. He wished that he still had a razer phone so that he could angrily shut it closed. These touch screens made it difficult for him to dramatically hang up on someone.

"So, you don't know where he lives?" Fran pouted. Her fight against the painful charlie horse was now over. She'd declared herself the victor against her own body.

"Not a clue," Catgatha said. "He moved to a fancy high rise next to the merchant mart," she continued. "That's about all I know."

Death's fingers moved quickly against tis phone screen. He was careful not to chip pieces of glass since it already had a large crack running diagonally from one end to another. The top right part of the screen was shattered, and tiny parts of glass were coming off of it. The pieces of glass resembled dozens of very small diamonds. He was trying to hold off from buying a new phone because he was anxiously waiting for the next version to come out, and he didn't want to have to settle for the same type of phone when he could get something that looked exactly the same for twice the money.

God: can you tell me why there are millions of aimless human souls wandering about earth? You know what? I'm calling you.

Death's phone buzzed. He sent the call to voicemail.

God: Nuh uh. You don't send me to voicemail, you son of a bitch.

"He must be making a pretty decent living if he could afford to live in the city," Fran said.

"Yeah. He just won the lottery with your soul,"Catgatha said.

Fran gave Catgatha a look of regret. She let out a soft whimper.

Death's phone continued buzzing. He tapped Fran's shoulder. "Hey, I'm gonna take a phone call. You got this, right? Yeah, you got it." He patted Fran on her forehead and walked away with his phone in his hand. It still buzzed, but he stalled to pick it up.

"I don't know exactly where he moved, but I can give you his old address. Maybe the new tenant can help you," Catgatha said lazily. She was beginning to lose interest in their conversation. Fran had already interrupted her plans of basking under the sun and taking naps all day. She gave Fran an address. It was in boys town. Fran raised an eyebrow.

"I didn't get that vibe from him," Fran said.

"Oh yeah. Big time. Frank's the gayest demon I've ever met," Catgatha explained.

"He gave off more of a toxic masculinity, asshole conman type of vibe. You know the one I'm talking about, right?"

Catgatha nodded. "I sure encountered enough of those in the army," she said. "Most of those guys are just closeted homosexuals. It's all for show. Frank is actually the head of the pride committee when he's not busy trying to rip people off."

Death inhaled deeply. His phone buzzed so violently that it rattled his boney hand. The sound of bones clanking from his hand sounded just like it did in cartoons. He cleared his throat and tapped on the green phone button on his cracked phone screen. "Death speaking."

"Get your boney ass up here. Now!" God said. The ground quaked around him as he commanded. The lighting lightninged above Death as he moved the phone away from his ear. He could feel God's warm, spitty breath from the speaker on his phone.

"Did you feel that?" Frank asked. Catgatha shrugged her shoulders. "I could have sworn that was an earthquake. Chicago never gets those. At least not as far as I know."

Death slumped his shoulders. A portal materialized in front of him. It released a bright, warm golden light. It radiated the feeling of a warm, loving embrace. Death realized he was in for a world of hurt. He took a step into the portal, and then dematerialized.

"Felt what?" Catgatha fought the urge to groom her crotch. She'd begun to lift her leg. Her tongue was out and halfway down to her crotch but stopped herself out of respect for Fran.

"Never mind. Thanks for the info." Fran reached to shake Catgatha's paw. She looked at her, puzzled, then extended her paw. Fran shook it with her thumb and her index finger and turned to walk back to her car.

"Hey, Dick. Ha, get it? Cause Richard's your name? wanna come with me to look for the face of Chicago's gay community?" She reached the mouth of the alley. Death was nowhere to be found.

137

Oh God.

Chapter 5:

Fran: Where'd you go?

Death: Duty Calls.

Fran: Disgusting. I don't want to know when you're poopin. Ha, duty. Are you coming back soon?

Death: Dunno.

Fran: Everything okay?

Death: Don't know yet. Dad's pissed. JK. It's God. He's throwing a tantrum.

Fran: K…

Death: K?

Fran:….

Fran:….

Fran:….

Death: GTG. To the principal's office I go.

Fran: Wait.

Death: What? Hurry..

Fran: I have a lead on Frank. Going to @#$% #

Death: What?

"You really stepped in it man." God bypassed the front desk. The door to his office slammed behind him. He ran his hands over his already messy hair. There was a five o'clock shadow developing on his chin. His eyes were bloodshot from too many energy drinks. Death could see a vein poofing up on the left side of his forehead. The last time Death had seen God, God had a full head of hair. Now he was showing signs of balding and had a very noticeable receding hair line. His secretary had just looked up from her monitor as God barreled past her. The waiting area was grandiose. Everything, from the floors to the ceiling, was made of the finest marble earth side of the universe. God was a big believer in buying local, and from small businesses. He was nothing short of a rich white kid with expensive taste, but he masked it in the form of being pro small business. So, he hit up his contact on the moon, Europa, who then hooked him up with Gene, a small-time miner who had quality marble for a great price. And, if one asked nicely, and wasn't a cop, he also offered the highest of quality weed. God would commission Gene's extracurricular services from time to time after their initial interaction. To start, however, God gave Gene a copy of the blueprint of his office, and since he was buying a huge amount of materials, and also contracting Gene's construction business, he was quoted a price well below market value. His secretary's desk alone was worth a whopping thirty million dollars as it was made from the purest of diamonds. Diamonds which Gene has mined with the help of children in Africa because they could get into tighter, much deeper spaces than their adult counterparts. The place was decorated with Greek God busts on top of Greek style pillars. There was an oil painting of God and his parents above the fireplace. It was rather pretentious. God sat in the middle of a golden thrown, on which sat a high thread cushion providing support for his celestial's butt. It had spectacular lumbar support. The whole thing was handcrafted in Italy. His parents stood on either side of him. God's dad, Jeffrey, had a hand resting atop God's left shoulder. His mom's hand rested on his right. They had a look on their face that indicated an air of arrogance as if to say *yes, we like to go endangered animal species hunting, and we keep their heads above our grand fireplace as a trophy.* Sort of like that one dentist that was caught killing lions and posing with them once they were dead. The only thing missing was a crown, but Death was sure that there was a version of it sitting around somewhere. If it were up to God, he would have worn a crown. However, HR felt it would have sent the wrong message. After all, God was supposed to exude a level of modesty that didn't require flashy items to reflect his social standing.

"Can you explain to me. Why is it that there are millions. No, billions of souls roaming around aimlessly down on earth? Like I mean, piling up, county dump style, one on top of the other, wandering on their own?" God's nostrils flared wildly each time he inhaled or exhaled. The vein on his forehead was now accompanied by a vein on his neck that was twice the size. It appeared as though it were about to pop. Death stared at it in disgust, and worry. He didn't want to have to clean blood off of his robe. Although his robe was black, and blood would most likely not stain it, he would know that the blood of God was caressing his garbs. Also, dry cleaning had gotten too expensive, and he was no longer able to add that as a business expense. President trump made it so that he couldn't add to many things as tax deductions. If God would have been human, both protruding veins would have exploded by now. Fortunately for him, and Death, he was immune to any mortal ailments, including the bursting of vicious looking veins. Death took the rout of ignorance and shrugged his shoulders. He pointed his palms toward God as an innocent gesture of his lack of this knowledge.

"Thank you for calling God. Can I take a message? He's a little busy at the moment," His secretary cut through the tension. Her professionalism was second to none, or at least it appeared as such. She knew Death was in for it, so she set up her phone in a concealed spot so that she could record the hot gossip. She was really hoping he'd get smitten by God's thunderbolts.

"God turned to priscilla, his secretary. "Thank you priscilla. That will be all," he said.

"Anything you need, sir." She avoided eye contact with Death, yet she looked at him as if to know he were dead meat.

"How about you take the rest of the day off," God told her.

"You're so kind, sir, but there's too much for me to do here," Priscilla said. She placed her hands on her hips and looked directly at her camera phone. "You need me now more than ever," she continued as she reached to hold

God's hand in support, which was odd because she'd never been the touchy feely type.

"Come with me," God barked at Death. He held his hands together in front of him, sort of like he was plotting something evil. His face grew a grim grin. Death looked down, like a sad child, as he made his way into God's even more grandiose office. "Sit," God huffed. The guy wore a neatly kept full beard. His hair was longer than shoulder length were it to fall straight down. He liked to regularly lift weights, so his muscles pressed tightly against his silk button down shirt. God's physique was a mixture of super lean and bulky. It was a rather difficult aesthetic to keep up with. Death, however, could see the very noticeable muscle definition over his shirt. God's office made the foyer look like a homeless man's shack in comparison. The wall behind him had a single, ten feet by eight foot, painting of him reigning over his kingdom. Death sat.

———————————————

Eric hesitated to walk up to Athena's office. After a lengthy inner struggle, he found it within himself to walk in and ask if he could maybe, possibly, go home early. Just a few hours. Not, like, the whole day. Not only had he not gone on a vacation in over ten years of service to Athena (which, as a result, he had accrued a significant amount of paid time off), his immune system had never given him an excuse to ask for a day off, preventing him having to ask. So, Athena (a no-nonsense woman who'd built up a construction empire after her dad nearly burned the business to the ground, who, then suddenly died after eating a bad batch of recalled romaine lettuce. It contained exorbitant levels of e coli mixed with anthrax. Athen then took it upon herself to revamp her dead dad's company. Her ability not to think twice about ruining the lives of anyone who ever thought about looking at her the wrong way gave her an added edge. Not only was she ruthless, but she was also beyond the level of sexy anyone had ever seen. It was almost Goddess like. Somehow, even as an insanely busy business entrepreneur, she found time in her schedule to win some of the most prestigious beauty pageants in the world. This left her employees terrified of her ruthless reputation, while also feeling an oppressive amount of horniness around her) would surely be sympathetic of him, notice his sacrifices and dedication to the company, and allow him to take the rest of the day off.

Before he knew it, Eric had found himself inside of Athena's office. She sat behind an unassuming desk, which was odd considering she was probably a billionaire, and surely had enough money for a fancy desk. Eric thought she was more modest than she let on, despite only wearing five-thousand-dollar business suits, coupled with a ten-thousand-dollar watch, and a fourteen thousand dollar, real elephant skin purse.

She appeared not to have noticed Eric stepping in. He stood in front of her office, with his hands near his hips, playing with his dusty, dark blue Athena building Co. hat. He fidgeted with it nervously, the fact that she didn't notice him wasn't surprising to Eric. He'd never been the noticeable type. People tended to forget him even being in the same room next to them, even if he was one of three people occupying the same room. "Hi, miss Athena," he said. He faced the ground where he stood atop a dirty tan carpet. It had dirt and oil stains all over it. Athena continued looking through a pile of paperwork. She opened bent up metal drawers from tall filing cabinets, some of which struggled to pry open even when she was pulling with all her force.

"Goddamnit! Of all fucking days!" she said. Her tight business pencil skirt made it difficult for her to maneuver easily around the small office space. It was even more difficult with her six-inch heels. Eric took a step back. He jolted as she forcefully shut the drawers. They made a loud clanking sound.

"I Can come back if it's too much of a problem. I don't mean to add to your stress," he said. His voice was soft, and humble. Eric sniffed a few times as though he were struggling with a pesky cold. Athena continued searching frantically. Off in the distance, Eric could hear the faint wail of sirens slowly getting louder. Athena now stood next to her chair, after failing in her search for her paperwork. Her cell phone rang.

"I think he's dead." Her hands made a dead gesture.

How can someone so beautiful be so intimidating, Eric thought.

"Call his family, but, for the love of God, don't make it sound like this was in any way our fault," Athena yelled into her phone. Her face remained unstrained, but he could sense the very real frustration coming out of her voice. Her red lipstick added to the illusion of her goddess like appearance. If he didn't know any better and was lucky not to have to work with her, but simply have passed by her on the street, he could have fallen in love with her at first sight if not for having been married to Jesenia, his wife of twenty years.

"Seems like you have your hands full," he said as he said. He had a creeping suspicion that he now might be complicit of a cover up. Eric wished he'd never walked in on that conversation. He didn't want to have to testify in court in front of a grieving family. He felt a blanketing feeling of sadness for whoever she was talking about. He mourned for whoever died while working for her. No one should have to die at work. This, he felt, should be something where the person dies surrounded by his loved ones as they reminisce about their lives together. Now he felt guilty for going to her for his seemingly small issue of having a runny nose. The sirens were now at their loudest. Almost as though they were on the site construction property. Red flashing lights entered the work site. He could see the paramedics through a window on the office door as they exited the ambulance with a stretcher the second it stopped. Two fire engines landed behind the ambulance shortly after, along with a small cavalry of CPD squad cars. At the very end of the convoy was a coroner's vehicle. The paramedics transported a motionless body covered by a white sheet back toward the ambulance. His coworkers stood curiously around, trying to catch a glimpse of the tragedy. Cops rushed to keep them from getting too close to the first responders. From where he stood, Eric could see that the white sheet was covered in a thin layer of dust, but he couldn't tell which one of his colleagues was under the sheet. He exited the trailer where Athena hid. He then walked toward the emergency vehicle, past the neatly groomed police officers. Some wore moustaches. The women kept their hair in a tight ponytail. They all had the same looking uniform, with the only difference being their rank. Some were sergeants, others were corporals. Some didn't have any rank insignia whatsoever. Not one of them paid any attention to Eric as he moved toward the motionless body. Eric then lifted the sheet off of his colleague's face, and he couldn't help but to think that the man who laid before him had a striking resemblance to himself. Then he noticed a bracelet his wife had gifted him for their anniversary a couple of nights before, which is when he realized that the doppelganger on the stretcher was him.

"There's no pulse!" said one of the paramedics as she held Eric's wrist. The other first responder cut through Erics clothing with a pair of sharp trauma sheers. He then placed a series gelatinous looking sticky pads connected to an array of wires, which were connected to a machine the size of a small box with a green screen on it. Presumably, it was used for telling whether their patients had heart beats and shocking them back into rhythm if they'd found themselves in a state of atrial fibrillation. In this case, Eric's heart wasn't even beating, confirming the female paramedic's diagnosis.

"Take him to the coroner's rig," the female paramedic said. Her name was Stacy, as it was displayed on her tattered name tag. Her face looked as tired and broken as the name tag above her left upper breast. Despite her state of fatigue, she gave off a gentle caring vibe that made Eric feel a warmth in his chest he wasn't sure where it was coming from. Stacy looked at Eric's motionless body, saddened by the tragedy. She'd been a paramedic since right after she graduated from high school. Unlike most of her friends, who went off to big four-year universities, she took a six-month paramedic class at her local community college and passed with nothing less than straight As. She had seen more tragedy in her short five years in the back of the ambulance than any of her friends, at any given time, combined. Suffice it to say, she was tired of seeing people die. Erick walked alongside his body and the paramedics.

"Don't know who you were, but I hope you rest easy," Stacy said in a hazed state. The paramedics helped the coroner load Eric's body into the back of his van.

At the hospital, Eric's body found a home at the morgue, on top of a cold metal table. He lay naked and motionless. His body almost didn't seem real to him. He felt that whoever was laying on the table could open his eyes at any moment and step off, wondering where all of his clothes had gone. His face had turned purple, along with several other parts of his body as a result of a brick wall having fallen directly on top of him. The blood below his skin was now pooling due to the lack of circulation. He was stiff. His body. Eric looked at his own ghostly hand and realized that he was transparent. He was wearing the torn-up uniform he was wearing when the accident happened, except they weren't torn, nor were they dirty. He appeared to be immaculate, except for the fact that he was transparent. He didn't quite understand what was happening yet, despite the constant reminder of his death laying directly in front of him. All he knew was that he had just shared a ride with a dead mat that shared a striking resemblance to him. He watched as two people in white lab coats placed his body in a freezer.

"D'you just get here?" Eric heard from behind him. He nodded. A semitransparent man touched his shoulder, and Eric turned to see who it was. The man extended a ghostly arm. "I've been here for about a day, maybe two," the man continued.

Eric looked at his own hands. The transparency gave him the ghost equivalent of goosebumps. "What's going on here?" he asked. "Who are you?" he continued his inquiries.

"Name's Rob." The man's voice was gruff, but friendly. "I think we're dead," he said.

"Dead? What do you mean you think we are dead?" Eric asked.

"Like we punched our ticked type of dead. We kicked the bucket. Our clock ran out," Rob explained as best he could. Another ghostly man came out of the bathroom. The toilet flushed as the door closed behind him. He patted his hands against his blue transparent jeans.

"Why you scaring him, Rob. I'm sure he's crapped his pants enough already. He don't need you fucking around telling him about him being dead so many times."

"Don't listen to him. He's from the Bronx, and has a foul mouth," Rob assured. A doctor then walked directly through the New Yorker.

"I'm walking here!" The New Yorker said with a huge grin on his face, and his arms spread out in front of him as though to indicate that he was in fact walking here. "We don't actually say that in New York. It just felt appropriate because the asshole has no manners. Talking about walking through people 'n shit." His accent was very much from New York. Unless he was just a really good faker.

"What makes you think we are dead?" Eric asked.

"It's just a hunch. Oh, and I'm pretty sure that doctor there is balls deep in my chest as we speak," Rob said. His body lay naked on a similar cold metal bed. The doctor used a hack saw to cut through his thick sternum. Rob's chest began to peel open on each side, revealing his heart, and lungs, and other internal organs. The doctor fought an itch on his nose. Instead, he scrunched his nose up and down and called it a day with the itch. Eric winced at the sound of the breaking bones coming from Rob's lifeless body. "It aint too bad," he said. "But I feel like we were lied to when they told us we'd get to see a bright light and shit."

"Those son's a bitches," the New Yorker said.

———————————

Fran: Why are the gays so well put together?

Death: Shh

Fran: Their crosswalks are rainbows!

Death: Fireworks emoji.

Fran: This neighborhood is so cute! None of the guys here have even stared at my ass! I can't tell if I'm offended or not.

Death: Shut up!

"Is there something more important that you need to take care of?" God asked from across his desk. Death shook his head. A cup of water on his desk was sweating profusely with condensation. The condensation turned into wine as it hit the desk below it. Death then noticed a large collection of water stains on the hard wood desk. He winced as he thought about how much God was ruining a magnificent piece of work.

"I've got it covered," Death replied in his most pseudo confident voice he could muster.

"Really? Because rumor has it, you've been dicking around doing God know what for the past few days," God yelled. He crossed his arms, and his muscular chest puffed out, giving him the appearance of having really firm, but muscular boobs. He even had a good amount of cleavage.

"And now I'm here," Death made his best attempt at a joke, and at diffusing the thick tension in the room.

"Don't be a wise ass," God said.

Death hesitated to tell him the truth. How was he going to explain that he was helping his human track her soul, and that she is willing gave away to one of the devil's minions, to God. With a capital G. "Okay, fine," Death cracked under the pressure. "I may, or may not, have hired a startup geek named Sanjeet, a really nice guy, to build an AI for me to take care of a few souls for me from time to time," Death admitted, quietly, as if this were any better than telling him about Fran. He shrank deep into his seat as he explained. God's face only appeared more enraged. His breathing was heavy with anger.

God sat silently, putting his thumb and his index finger on the bridge of his nose. He leaned back on his chair as if he were thinking of ways in which he could fuck Death up. His body language was scarier than if he were screaming. At least, if he were to scream as he usually did, Death knew exactly where he stood in terms of being erased from all existence. The yelling was a good sign that there was still room to bullshit his way out of the problem. This silence was something else entirely. This meant that he was weighing his options. He could go crazy and decide to erase him from existence. Even worse, he could decide to wipe out Death's pension, which by now was at a really good point. God took a sip of water. The ice inside the cup clinked against the glass as he raised it to his lips. Death glared at a collection of water stain rings and thought *how God can be so terrible. The act alone of desecrating the desk was blasphemy in and of itself.*

"Do you remember," God paused. He placed the cup down.

Fran: This guy Frank has good taste.

Death. Not now!

Fran: you should see this town house. The new guys said Frank completely renovated the brick siding. The inside is to die for.

Death: You're killing me.

Fran: These are my kind of people.

Death: Gay?

Fran: No. Educated and cultured. So, what if they are gay.

Death: Nothing is wrong with being gay.

Fran: Then why mention it.

Death: I was trying to clarify.

Fran: You're a homophobe.

Death: Am not.

Fran: What if I told you I was gay.

Death: I'd say "cool."

God slammed his hands on the desk. Remember about twenty five years ago. I sent you to Chicago General Hospital to collect the soul of Margarette Morrow?" Death nodded. His fingers moved quickly against his phone's screen. "Put that down," God said. Death dropped the phone onto his lap. "Then remember how I had said, "Richard, she's ninety years old and has about an hour left on earth. Do you remember that, Death?" God continued his interrogation.

"Yes. She was a lovely lady," Death said.

"Sir," Priscilla's head peaked into the room. She made no effort to knock before opening the door, a habit God didn't care much for. God took in a deep breath. His large, muscular chest moved out and back in as he tried his best to keep calm. His jaw tensed.

"Yes, priscilla?" God said with gritted teeth.

"Your mom called and asked if you're still on for dinner later tonight," Priscilla said. She blew a pink bubble until it popped and slurped it back into her mouth.

Death twiddled his thumbs. He turned toward his lap to check for any more incoming text messages from Fran. A ray of sun entered through a window beside him, revealing an even larger collection of liquid stain in the shape of a ring on God's desk.

"Can you please tell my lovely mother I will head over to the Ritz and meet up with her and dad as soon as

I'm done with work?" He maintained a menacing stare upon Death.

"And sir," Priscilla continued.

"Yes, Priscilla?" God's voice was now considerably less patient with his nosey secretary.

"Should I cancel your one o'clock?" God turned toward her direction, giving Death a small reprieve from his soul crushing glare, which was now reserved for Priscilla. "Very well sir. I will have RBG come back at a later date," She said.

"When did that happen?" Death asked.

"When did what happen?"

"RBG."

"What do you mean RBG. You brought her here last week." God said. Drops of spit landed directly on top of Death's lips. He dry heaved discreetly so as to not annoy God any further. "You're literally going to give me a heart attack. Don't think I forgot what I was talking about, either. What, better said, who did you bring me when I asked for the ninety-year-old woman all those years ago?"

Death became overwhelmed with a high level of shame and embarrassment that he had never experienced in his short billion years of existence.

"Did he say ninety-year-old? Or nine days old. Shit."

Fran was scheduled to be released later that day. The doctors had decided to monitor for a little longer than they would another baby because she had been born a month before she was supposed to and was deathly underweight. They feared that her immune system wouldn't be strong enough to support her outside of a non-sterile environment. Death hated having to report back to God if ever he had a chance to avoid it. From an outsider's perspective, Fran's fragile little body was just as likely to expire as well as that of a ninety-year-old, terminally ill cancer patient. However, Death happened to be on a time crunch, and had no time to waste. He had purchased tickets to watch the blue man group in downtown Chicago, and he was not about to miss the show again. Not after spending three hundred dollars on the tickets. If he counted the show he missed, he was out over six hundred dollars. He looked at Fran's chart, and figured she must have been his assignment based on her being a preemie. "Sorry little one," he said, and collected her soul.

Fran thrived in the afterlife. She quickly gained weight. Excelled in all the milestones a baby had to excel at, at the exact moment they had to. At the prime age of five, she had skipped pre-school and went straight on to first grade. She was very popular early on. Her spirit parents were the most supportive spirit parents a spirit little girl could ever ask for. After she graduate from high school, she moved to after life New York where she studied at Juilliard School of Dace. From there, she booked a gig on Broadway where she performed on a regular basis as a recent college graduate. She never married but was surrounded by a family that she chose and loved in the form of life-long friends, and, of course, her spirit parents. By ninety, she was the most well-respected playwright in the country. Until one day, after something bothered Death enough to look further into her life file, he realized he'd made a terrible mistake. Quietly, he wrangled Fran's soul, and tossed it back into the tiny baby body she had been ripped from. Fran had only been officially dead for an entire twelve seconds before the medical staff were able to bring her back.

"It's a miracle we brought her back!" the doctors would say. Death walked out of the hospital that day as though no harm had been done. He just wished he didn't hadn't given the baby too much brain damage.

———————————————

"Oh yea. I wondered what ever happened to that baby!" Death said Cheerfully.

"No fucking clue," God said. "What I do know is that you never brought Margarette Morrow back! She's still out there, after all these years!" God released a spry of spit now.

"How? Her cancer was terminal," Death said.

"Without you guiding her soul, her body never died."

"Good for her!" Death cheered.

God threw his cup at the wall. He considered chucking it directly between Death's eyes, but he didn't want to have to deal with HR over an assault and battery. What could they do to him, anyway. He was God. He regretted choosing the wall as the cup's target. Now he had to worry about getting someone in after hours to get the stains out of his pristine white wall. The cup shattered into hundreds of little pieces too. The explosive cup drenched Death with water and wine, and small shards of glass.

"I've chosen to turn a blind eye to your fuck ups, Death. I can't keep cleaning up your messes," God said.

"I didn't chuck the cup at the wall, sir," Death said sheepishly. The ray of sun shining brightly into God's office retreated in fear behind a thick, grey cloud that darkened the room.

Fran: Okay, I have a game plan.

Death: Please. Not now. Dad is angry. Smiley emoji.

Fran: I have a rough idea where Frank lives, but it's not going to be easy.

"Can I see that?" God pointed at Death's phone resting on his lap.

"Oh this? It's the new iPhone fifteen," Death said excitedly. "I got it as a part of a promotion. Guess how much it cost me," he asked.

"How much?" God asked as Death handed him the phone. He seemed genuinely interested.

"Free! If you go in now, I can see if they could hook you up with a good deal," Death said conversationally.

"You'd do that for me?" God asked in faux excitement. He turned the phone over in his big meaty hands as if to closely inspect it.

"Of course I would. Anything for you."

"Great, great," God said. Then he squeezed the phone as tightly as he could, breaking it into a million little pieces, and chucked it at the exact location his cup full of water turned to whine had landed, nearly hitting Death in the head if not for him ducking fast enough. "I don't care what dumbass geek you hired to do your job!" God emphasized the word your. Death was sure that the vein on God's forehead was going to explode any second now. "Fix it! "God said with a ferocity of a trillion burning suns. You're lucky it's me that you're dealing with right now." If my mom and dad find out about the billions of souls being backed up down on earth, not only will they kill me, but they will make sure that they tear you apart, atom by atom, making sure to rip your scrotum out in the most painful way possible." Death moved his hands toward his crotch. He gulped. "I'm glad we have an understanding," God said.

165

The Devil Drinks Glacier Water.

Chapter 6:

Frank's New apartment sat on the highest floor of an iconic Chicago high rise. The apartment itself was small and had only one room. So, a studio apartment. The walls, and the décor with which it was pre furnished were mind-numbingly neutral. Frank immediately started making plans for a full renovation the moment he turned the key to his new home. The place wouldn't be truly his until his queer eye had a chance to give the place a well needed face lift. The view had been what sold him into signing the lease and committing to an ungodly amount of money per month on rent, which, after having collected his earnings by selling Fran's soul, the idea of being able to afford a lake view was no longer unattainable. His pad had a complete view of Navy Peer, allowing him to catch a glimpse of the regular display of fireworks the peer hosted during the summertime.

Frank sat on his couch in the living room. He looked out the floor to ceiling window that doubled as a wall. "Thanks for the advance, boss," he said. He kicked his feet up onto a sheik, modern looking coffee table.

Despite being forced to live with pre-furnished furniture, the place was rather minimalistic. His sinuses felt unusually clear now that he didn't have to share a living space with Catgatha.

The devil held the phone receiver tightly. He was a fair believer in using a landline because he could tell the quality of service was much better, and a whole lot more reliable than that of a cell phone. He tried to use a cell phone once before but had too many issues with getting service. Calls would regularly drop in the middle of important meetings, contrary to what the big cell phone companies said about their service being top notch, even in the depths of hell. Their claims of five G being a good fit for his business were completely bogus. Only one group of people shared a similar sentiment. Those were the ones that opted for vinyl records over digital soundtracks when it came to listening to music. They also had a tendency to like more culturally highbrow music, which definitely earned those people some amount of brownie points when it came to being on the Devil's good side. Landline lovers, and vinyl enthusiasts were generally treated a little better during their stay in hell. Their registration upon entering was certainly a better experience than most. This was all very common knowledge within the entrails of hell. Most didn't like it, but the Devil didn't care. They were there to pay for their sins, not to make friends. God have mercy on one's soul if the Devil caught someone pretending to share common interests, though. He had a knack for sniffing out posers. He had a special place for people like that. However, if you weren't being tortured for such transgressions, and say you were the demon assigned to disciplining the worst offenders (posers), then you needed a higher than top secret security clearance to be privy to what went on during the disciplining of posers.

"Don't mention it," The Devil played with the red, curly chord attached to the receiver on his phone.

"Really, boss. Thanks so much," Frank said breathlessly as he sat peacefully on his couch.

"I'm serious. Don't mention it. This is the first soul you have transferred in over two hundred years. I should have melted you," the Devil said in a smooth, deep yet reassuring tone.

Frank imagined his skin peeling off at the mention of being melted. "Kids are much smarter than they used to be," he said as he pulled on his shirt collar.

"The last soul you brought me was a stolen one," the Devil said skeptically. He had sworn to himself that he was never to trust Frank again after that, but business had been recently very slow.

Magda, the Devil's secretary, knocked on his office door. She waited a moment before he allowed her in. The screams of trillions of tortured souls flood into his office as she opened the door. The light from the outside, a warm crimson red, infiltrated every knock and cranny within the office. Unexpectedly, the interior of his office was tastefully decorated. Very modern, with neutral colors too. He had made sure to tell his interior designer he wanted something modern, but not pretentious, yet timeless. There were long Palestinian drapes hanging gracefully against the windows. They'd been gifted to him by Palestinian royalty. A big screen T.V hung off the wall across from him where he would catch up on current events in the morning before starting his busy workday. A pristine, black, dragon leather couch accented the room with just the right amount of class. A beautiful, red stained with a glossy finish, sleek, African blackwood desk was home to an unreleased, thirty-inch, apple computer monitor, along with the apple accoutrement. Behind him, the wall was adorned with several higher education degrees and diplomas. One being his credentials from Harvard Law, and a Ph.D. in string theory and advanced physics from the Massachusetts Institute of Technology. The Devil himself, despite nursing the worst hangover in the existence of hangovers, wore a classy, three-piece suit that was personally tailored for him by non-other than Savile Row Tailors who only cater to highly respected clients such as the English royalty (one may recognize King Charles III, perhaps.) The Devil was also the biggest wristwatch enthusiast and refused to wear anything other than the most expensive of Rolex's.

"Not now, please, Magda," The Devil said. The screams from the tortured souls made his already pudding-like brain further decay into a pile of unrecognizable mush. He covered his eyes. The light from the fiery hellscape nearly made his eyeballs explode.

"Sir, it's corporate," Magda said.

"They can wait." The Devil gagged. The urge to vomit came quickly. He dashed toward the toilet as puke was going to exit him imminently. He narrowly avoided throwing up over his desk.

"Very well, sir. I shall tell them to fuck off," Magda said, in no uncertain terms.

"Thanks, Magda." The Devil covered his eyes with one hand and waved her off with the other. The crippling sounds disappeared instantly the moment his devilish secretary closed the door. Everyone thought he was insane when he suggested sound proofing all the offices and spending a little more on quality Palestinian blackout curtains after the royals had only given him only one set for free. Even the assholes in corporate loved their quiet cubicles, except there was absolutely no way they would ever admit that the Devil himself had come up with a brilliant idea like that. Instead, they found a way to take credit, making themselves out to be the heroes of the underworld. None of them thought he was capable of having good ideas, despite the fact that on his wall hung a grand collection of high-level education degrees. Does being the first college graduate in his family not mean anything these days?

"Yo, Lucy," he heard from the other end of the receiver. He rolled his eyes, remembering that he was still talking with his detestable friend, Frank.

"Sorry, my bloody secretary, God bless her soul, just walked in here, letting all the screams in," he said as he made his way back from the office bathroom. He massaged his temples. His tongue was beginning to feel dry, and coarse. He made smacking noises with his mouth as if to confirm the dryness in his mouth.

"I certainly don't miss those screams," Frank said. He picked at his toes while holding the phone against his shoulder. The nail clippings flew to the opposite end of his small apartment. Frank had a tendency to do a good amount of self-grooming whenever he had any conversations over the phone that were anything longer than thirty seconds.

"Yeah, well, not everyone's a traitor like you, and dip whenever a young piece of ass bats his eyelashes at him," the Devil said. He reached towards the mini fridge below his desk and clumsily searched for a glass bottled glacial water that had been collected directly from the melting icecaps in Antarctica.

"We broke up a while ago. Turns out he wasn't really a gay dude. I caught him cheating on me with one of his female coworkers. Apparently, he decided that boobs, real ones, not like my man boobs, were a lot nicer to look at," Frank said. He looked disappointed. He wasn't as over Rodrigo as he thought he was.

"I'm terribly sorry, Frank. If there's anything I can do just let me know. Don't take my sympathy as the same thing as me not hating you. You still owe me for that stolen soul two hundred years ago. I only gave you an advance because your mom is my aunt, and I love your mom. She always calls me during the holidays. Do you call me during the holidays, Frank? I didn't think so."

"Don't worry about it. It was amicable. It would have been shitty of me to force him to stay, although I could have. He's a puny human. I could have mended him to my apartment and never let him go. Then I could have forced him to love me for all eternity, while torturing him for being a dick," Frank was flustered.

"Is that really what you did? Let him go just like that?" The Devil asked. He didn't know Frank to be much of a softy.

"Okay, fine. No. I tore his spine out of his body and used it as a centerpiece for my place. Then I weighted his body with concrete and threw it in the middle of the ocean, near where you used to dump cadavers shortly after you became the devil. His spine is still in my living room. I wanted to keep a nice souvenir," Frank explained. He was very proud of his centerpiece spine. It was usually a conversation starter whenever he had company over. He'd happily say that it used to belong to his boyfriend, and his house guests would laugh it off as though he were joking. Even when he'd follow up by telling them that he wasn't actually lying. Then they'd stare at each other quietly until someone else had the common sense to change the topic to something less incriminating, like stocks.

"That sounds more like it," the Devil said. He placed the cold, glass, glacial water bottle up to his forehead and let out a sigh of relief. The coolness felt amazing against his hot and dry skin.

"Also, this soul is legit. I got her on camera saying she was a completely willing participant. I didn't even bring her to my leather couch," Frank said. He was still kicking himself over not even trying.

"Did you have her sign all the release forms? All the legal mumbo jumbo? More importantly, the waiver that states we own her likeness forever and in perpetuity. I haven't received the fax," the Devil asked. He placed the bottle back onto his desk. Frank jumped from his seat and faxed the document. He ruffled over a pile of open mail until he found a stack of paperwork with Fran's name on it, presumably a contract. He didn't remember having her sign it but sent the documents over regardless. The fax in the Devil's office started making a loud noise until it spit out formerly clear papers now with legalese. "I see it coming in now. Broadband must be a little saturated.

"Yeah, the broadband." Frank scratched his head. "Who do you use?" he asked shamelessly. The hairs on the back of his chunky neck stood at attention. Paranoia began to set in about Fran breaking in and asking for her soul back. He hoped that she didn't somehow figure out where he had moved to.

"Some tiny startup in San Francisco. Some geek named Sanjeet was advertising his services on craigslist that emphasized the fact that he was well versed with celestial matters."

"You don't say." Frank walked around his apartment in nothing but underwear. Then he made his way toward the front door as he picked a wedgie that was lodge deeply between his butt cheeks. He peeped through the peephole.

The Devil popped open a bottle of ibuprofen and made sure not to go over the daily recommended dose. He downed the pills with one swift motion and chased it with a fresh drink of delicious glacial water. He felt as the icy water traveled down his throat and into his stomach. The liquid, mixed with the acids triggered a gaseous reflex within his stomach. A belch escaped him, rattling the golden chandelier in the foyer. "Oof. Excuse me," he said. "Yeah. He gave me a really good deal. Okay. Good," said the Devil. He picked up the release form, along with the title of her sou and placed it inside one of his desk drawers without having a lawyer look over the paperwork. He could have also done it himself since he'd passed the bar exam, but he was in no condition to read over a mountain of documents that had extremely small print. His reading glasses were nowhere in sight. He wondered if maybe he'd forgotten them at home. He really hoped they weren't lost because his insurance wouldn't cover a new pair for another six months, and he couldn't go without his glasses, or else it would be impossible for him to read. "Anyway, Magda is blowing up my phone. If anything, and I mean anything, comes back crooked with that soul I'm going to kill you. Not just kill your human host. I'll tear your demon essence into a billion pieces, then put you through a pulverizer until there's nothing left. We can't afford to bleed money right now. Business has been too bad for any screw ups, and the dickheads are making me lay off my greatest, and most dishonest demons." He struggled to contain his rage. The phone in his hands began to crack from how tightly he was holding it.

"That can't be good," Frank said.

"No shit, skin bag." The Devil ran his fingers through his hair. The odor from his mouth had now caught up with him. He breathed hard into his open palm and jerked back from how bad his breath was. A combination of the highest proof vodka and rotten chimichangas escaped his mouth in a toxic cloud of mouth air. His head throbbed. The ibuprofen couldn't kick in fast enough. "All I'm saying is, if I have to lay more people off, more good men and women like Lamarck and Katina, I'm going to murder someone."

"Fuck no. Not those two."

"Yeah, it happened. If I have to do that, and I realize you're giving me any souls you didn't acquire by the fucken book, I'm grabbing you by the balls, and feeding them to my goldfish, Sasha." He pointed at his goldfish. It had a long strand of poop coming out of it. Sasha bumped into the glass wall in front of her repeatedly. The Devil looked at her with admiration.

"Message received," Frank said. The Devil slammed his phone and hung up. Frank looked at his screen to see he was no longer connected to the call. "Unbelievable," he said. The way the sun shined through his window made his chest hair even more visible. It was a thick mat of sweaty, curly hair. The door then thumped. Three police like thumps emanated from it. His body fought against itself. It couldn't decide between opening the door, or rushing to get some clothes before he opened it. The thumping continued. They rattled his entire apartment. He turned toward his room, then toward his front door a few times as though he'd glitched until finally he involuntarily asked who it was. "Don't know how she did it," he mustered to himself and opened the door as he wore nothing but underwear.

An eighteen-year-old kid holding a pizza greeted him. He wore a blue uniform, and a red hat. There was a small patch of hair growing where a beard would grow. His face was full of pimples at every stage of growth and decay. His nose was covered with blackheads. His face was greasy, which explained the state of his acne ridden skin.

"Who the hell are you?" Frank looked at him up and down. "Oh shit. Hold on." He ran in a way an elderly man that had both hip and knee problems would toward his room. The pizza guy could have lived his entire life completely happily if he didn't have to see the huge piece of fabric missing from his underwear over his butt. Franks butt left butt cheek, and presumably his right, had even thicker curly hairs than his chest. It was like looking at a black, unkept, fuzzy sheepskin carpet. The reality was that the kid lived in an imperfect world. One in which he'd catch a glimpse or two of hair old men's butts every now and again, especially if they were as shameless as Frank. This experience would serve him well, though, as he would use it as fuel to go on to be one of the most successful attorneys in the United States of America. The pizza kid would go on to help legislate a pivotal bill outlawing old men from answering the door to pizza delivery men, and women, and anyone who had to deliver anything to people's residences, in their underwear. His bill was revered as some of the most important pieces of legislation the nation had ever seen. His second most famous work was one that made it a requirement for businesses to pay delivery people a lofty hazard fee when on deliveries. This came as a result, mostly because he'd been shot by a four-year-old with a nerf gun almost a year before being the victim of Frank's assault to his eyes. Frank returned with a wadded-up pile of cash, still in his underwear. The cash only covered the cost of the pizza. The delivery kid would be the first to say that A). The view upon Frank's return was as repulsive as when he walked away from him, and was enough to make a blind person puke, and B) not tipping was simply just rude.

Tech Whiz.

Chapter 7:

Sanjeet liked to live a modest life. He grew up in India, with his mother and father, both of which were respected, highly adored doctors in their hometown. Like many good parents, they wished to provide their only child with nothing but the best of niceties and opportunities they'd lacked while they were growing up. While his mother, Sunee was pregnant, his father and her agreed that living in an area with a better school district would give their unborn son the tools that he'd need in order to follow in their footsteps and become a doctor.

Unfortunately for Sunne, and his father Ragu, Sanjeet took a keen liking, more of an obsession, with everything involving technology. Sanjeet would regularly disassemble and reassemble any piece of technology his parents had owned. At first, such exercises would end up in the trashing of their devices. However, the more he practiced, the more skilled Sanjeet became. He slowly became more capable at putting things back together as though he'd never taken them apart in the first place.

Although his parents disagreed with his passions, saying things like "one only chooses the tech industry as a backup. There is no future in technology. No one ever became rich and famous from it," the words were still fresh in his mind to this day, Sanjeet found a passion within himself that wouldn't allow him to think about anything other than creating things with computers.

"I'm leaving to San Francisco," He told them one day. "And I'm opening a startup!" He would say to them. Sanjeet's parents decided to shun him for this blatant display of disrespect.

"If you walk out that door, you are no longer part of the Gupta family," his father told him on the day he had chosen to move.

"You don't get it! Technology is my passion, dad!" Sanjeet yelled at the top of his lungs. His mother stood silently crying next to her husband as he and Sanjeet fought. Sanjeet was reaching for the door.

"Why can't you become a doctor, like me and your mom?" Ragu asked.

"That's not me. I'm going to create great things. Things that will help people."

"We help people, son. Not computers."

"I'll show you!" Sanjeet said and walked out the door.

In his tiny San Francisco apartment, Sanjeet downed his third can of red bull just before midnight. His heart raced at least two hundred beats per minute while sitting and staring at his computer screen. He wore anti blue light glasses to protect his eyes from the harmful light emanating from the screen, and even though his apartment was mostly dark, it gave his surroundings a sickly tint of yellow whenever he wore them. He was working on some advertising that targeted the likes of celestials. Now that he'd escaped Death, his ability to communicate with all sorts of supernatural beings turned into an opportunity to maximize his profitability, and he intended on cornering that market.

Death knocked on Sanjeet's door. Sanjeet cracked it open, using his weight to prevent would be trespassers from barging in. The smell of stale Doritos and body odor hit Death's nostrils. He placed his robe over his nose to prevent the foul odors from melting his brain. "What's the password?" Sanjeet asked. He gave the appearance of that of a drug dealer. He looked through the crack suspiciously.

"Open the door, geek," Death said impatiently. He tapped the heel of his foot rapidly against the carpeted floor in the hallway.

"You're mean," Sanjeet said. "I thought we agreed on this password thing," he said.

"I mean it, geek. Now open up." Death looked down the hall as if to check that no one was trailing him.

"Are you being followed?" Sanjeet asked.

"I'm not, fucking, Jason Bourne. No one is following me"

"Then why are you looking down the hallway expecting to be shot at by a Russian spy, or the CIA?" Sanjeet asked. He'd been watching the Bourne movies back-to-back recently. His imagination was running wild.

"That's none of your concern, now open," Death said. Sanjeet opened the door, but not without showing Death how disappointed he was that they didn't use a password.

The inside of Sanjeet's studio apartment was dark. Death could tell that Sanjeet had tried to mask the strong smell of body odor with what must have been axe body spray, but this just left the room smelling even worse, and chemically. Monitors with ones and zeroes took up half the living space. In the kitchen space, he had a coffee pot boiling water with instant ramen noodles in it.

"We had a deal," Death said. If he had nostrils they'd be flailing. "Do you know where I just came from? If you were there you would have shat your pants," he said angrily.

"Sanjeet took a seat on his three-thousand-dollar gaming chair. That was quite possibly the most expensive piece of furniture he'd owned. He mattress sat on top of milk crates, and he didn't own a couch. Sanjeet closed a window on his computer screen that had a picture of him, and poor depictions of different celestials. "Let me guess. Your mom's house?" Sanjeet asked.

"Maybe I'll just take you now. I'll tell the big guy your soul was corrupt, but I'm pretty sure you belong in hell anyway. You'd love it down there. All the assholes with no girlfriends go there," Death said. "You'd know all about that."

"Okay, let me take a look," Sanjeet said. Keyboard clinks clinked as quickly as his fingers could type. "Interesting," he said. He nodded. His eyebrows furled as though he were deep in thought. He continued typing quickly. Sanjeet moved the mouse beneath his frail brown hand dramatically and deliberately. Death crossed his arms. He pulled up his sleeve and looked at his watch. The watch's hands weren't moving, even the seconds hand was standing still. The concept of time had been distorted by traveling from the earthly plane to the celestial, and back. Losing functionality of his watch only made for a more annoying visit to Sanjeet after having been drilled a new butthole by God for Sanjeet's crappy automated program. The fact that Sanjeet kept his curtains shut further distorted Death's sense of time and added even more so to his frustration.

"Aha!" Sanjeet said. Death perked up. He uncrossed his arms and leaned in closer to the screen. The heavy feeling of his chest began to disappear.

"Please give me good news," Death said. He tried to get a better look. A window was opened to one of Sanjeet's favorite sub sandwich shops. He was looking at a tuna sub that admittedly looked very appetizing. Death's stomach rumbled at the sight. Regardless, he smacked Sanjeet on the back of his head.

Sanjeet lifted his arms as if to brace for another attack. "What? It's great news. It's hard to get good food delivered in this area. I'm always, "out of district," he said.

Death materialized his scythe. He looked at it, and rubbed a smudge off of it until the spot was shiny again.

"Okay, okay, jeeze," Sanjeet said. "Okay, so this is what happened," he explained. He leaned his char further back so that he could address Death better. "Turns out the program you had me make gained sentience."

"I don't understand," Death said. He used his scythe to lean on.

"I mean the program developed a mind of its own." Death nodded in understanding. "It apparently has a list of demands before it lifts a digital finger again," Sanjeet said. Death looked for signs of him lying, or trying to be funny, but he saw no indication that pointed at any sort of funny business occurring.

"You're fucking with me," Death said disinterested.

"I am not, my murdery friend."

Death huffed. Sanjeet reached for a Mountain Dew. He took a sip and gulped three big gulps. Then he belched loudly in the direction of Death's face. Death covered his nose in efforts to avoid breathing in the disruptive burp. "What are the demands?" Death asked. "Also, if you do that again, I'm going to kill you where you sit," he threatened.

"She. Her demands," Sanjeet corrected. He took another sip of his beverage. He looked at the screen to make sure that the now sentient computer program hadn't heard Death's insensitivity.

"Her demands, damnit." Death lifted both hands to his temples. The scythe dropped against a desk. He massaged his temples to relieve some tension, then took a seat on one of Sanjeet's computer CPUs.

"That's not a-" Sanjeet began to say.

Death pointed at his fallen scythe.

"Okay. Andrea Ignacious said."

"You named her?" Death asked incredulously. Of course he'd named her. The guy had no friends, and the idea of a sex partner was a blow-up doll with talking capabilities.

"No, she named herself. I told you; she is sentient."

"You're kidding me?"

"Wish I were, boss. Andrea's First demand is," Sanjeet leaned closer to the speaker. "I'm sorry, she is very quiet sometimes. She has a tendency to whisper," he said.

"Why don't you turn up the volume?"

Sanjeet lifted a finger as if to tell Death to be quiet. Death smacked his face. His hands slid down slowly.

"She wants us to be nicer to her, and for us to say please and thank you," Sanjeet said seriously. His face looked concerned for Andrea. He understood the feeling of being under appreciated and disrespected. He was experiencing that as he sat there in front of Death.

"Done, considering you're the only one who will be doing any talking. Stop being a dick to her," Death said.

"Her second demand is," Sanjeet leaned forward again. Death tapped at his wristwatch, hoping that it somehow started working again. He didn't want to have to spend any money to fix it, much less have to replace it entirely. The heel of his foot tapped even faster than it did when he was standing outside of Sanjeet's apartment.

"She wants an eight-hour workday, weekends and holidays off, and paid time off," Sanjeet relayed her demands.

"That's it?" Death asked in disbelief.

"Oh, and benefits," he said. "She really emphasized the benefits. She says she may want to have kids one day, and the cost of health care these days is too expensive to be able to pay out of pocket," he continued.

"Anything else?" Death asked. Sanjeet whispered. Andrea whispered back. It sounded like unintelligible computer noises.

"Now that you mention it. She wants a food stipend, and mileage reimbursement," Sanjeet said. "And also, a housing allowance. Prices for a good home in San Francisco have skyrocketed, and she doesn't want to have to pay a ton of money out of her paycheck just so that she could live in a rundown shack."

"For fuck's sake, Sanjeet, It's a fucking computer! A machine!" Death stood up enraged. "Tell that fucking thing to do its job like it was programed to, or I'll have her deactivated. Erased. Thrown away like a piece of garbage that she is," he continued. Sanjeet cut him off.

"Andrea," he said as he looked at the keyboard.

"Tell. Fuck… Tell Andrea I don't deal with terrorists, or unions. Either she does her job, or I have to erase her. As for you! Fix it!" Death demanded. A boney vein started to show above his eyebrow. He looked at Sanjeet. "If you don't fix this, I'm going to erase you too!" His eyes lit up in a fiery, blood red rage. "Also, I need a new phone," he said, now less intimidating, and more like a kid that's asking his parents for something he knew he'd get in trouble for asking for. "God pulverized mine, and I don't have time to go to AT&T. Give me yours." He reached for Sanjeet's phone, which was lying next to the keyboard. "I promise I will bring it back," he said and stormed out. He stormed back moments later because he forgot his scythe. He grabbed it from where it sat, on top of one of Sanjeet's desks, and stormed back out.

193

The Jig Is Up.

Chapter 8:

Death: Just got back. God is pissed. Anyway, where are you?

Not Fran: What?

Death: Oh, crap. Right. It's me, Death. New phone. Who dis? Lol.

Not Fran: Funny. Who is this? And why are you texting me?

Death: What do you mean who is this? It's me. Death.

Death:………

Death: Are you going to make me say it?

Not Fran: Say what?

Death: My name.

Not Fran: Yes! Who is this?

Death: God. I…

Death: Richard.

Not Fran: Richard who?

Death: You're fucking with me.

Death: Right?

Death: Yeah, you're fucking with me.

Death: (sends a selfie)

Not Fran: Cool costume bro.

Death: Stop jerking me around.

Not Fran: Okay. Sorry. What's up.

Death: Finally. Where are you?

Not Fran: Up your butt.

Death: No, really.

Not Fran: Up your mom's butt.

Death: You're so annoying.

Not Death: You've got the wrong number, asshole!

Death looked at the number he'd been texting the last digit was most definitely incorrect.

Death: Oh shit. Sorry. My bad.

Death: Fran?

Death: Who dis? New number.

Death looked back at the number. This time it was correct. He sighed with relief.

Death: It's me, Death.

Fran: Everything okay? What's with the new number?

Death: Long story. God pulverized mine in a fit of rage. I'll tell you about it later.

Fran: Face palm emoji

Death: Where you at?

Fran: Meet me at the bean.

Death: The coffee place? I could use some caffeine.

Fran. No. The big shiny thing at Millenium Park.

Death: What, are you a tourist? Next, you're going to call the Sears Tower, "The Willis Tower," like a jackass.

Fran: NEVER THAT!

Death: What's after that? You're going to put ketchup on your hotdogs?

Fran: I've never understood that. I like ketchup on my dog.

Death: That's why you have no friends. Are you also going to be one of those annoying people that say, "Dad Bears!" really obnoxiously?

Fran: I don't follow sports ball.

Death: Blasphemy!

Fran: Phone's dying. Meet you at the bean.

"There's so many people here," Fran said. Some teen kid stared at the bean intently. He inched his face slowly toward the bean. The reflection from the art installation reflected the kid's braces, and his curly hair.

"Don't look at me, you chose this place. I'm rather kind of liking it here," Death said. He watched as some eight-year-old kid ran across a flock of hungry pigeons. Feathers fell off of them as they dispersed in efforts to avoid being trampled. They quickly returned to eat the pieces of bread an hold homeless woman was tossing at them. The homeless woman's proud smile revealed a mouth that lacked the majority of her upper front teeth. A stolen shopping cart next to her contained the entirety of her earthly belongings. Death's intuition told him he either had to collect her soul soon, or he had completely missed the call asking him to claim her. He looked at his soul book. Since he didn't know her by name, he snapped a quick picture of her and cross referenced it with his database. Marry Louise, a former stock trader. The fifty-nine-year-old woman lost a fortune shortly after the great toilet paper shortage of twenty twenty. The few details in her file that revealed where she went wrong were murky at best. His soul database had mostly superficial information. It wasn't his business to know the person's life choices in detail. That job belonged to God, and the Devil. Anyway, her profile simply stated, "Any day now."

"I may have chosen it, but that doesn't mean I like it. I hate people," Fran said. Her gaze remained intently upon the brace faced, curly haired, chubby teen. He stuck his tongue out and turned his head side to side in an effort to avoid any glares from any known faces. One he was mostly sure that no one was watching, he pulled the trigger metaphorical trigger and licked the bean clean where he stood. The boy was thorough, to say the least. It was as though he were being paid to maintain its cleanliness. With one swift motion, he walked a few feet to his right with his tongue firmly affixed to the structure. He somehow avoided having bumped into any of the other tourists who stood there, admiring the magnificent work of art that was covered in bird poop at the time, and along the sides. The teenager left behind him a long, we, gooey streak of saliva as he moved from one side to the other. Never mind the fact that that surface had been touched by at least a few thousand people that morning, and that the art installation hadn't been cleaned since it was installed, back in two thousand and four. Unbeknownst to him, his father had been witnessing the entire event from across the way as he sat on a bench, not more than twenty feet away from him. His father immediately wondered where he'd gone wrong with his son.

"Have you ever been to boys town?" Fran asked. "Let's head out. Frank's apartment isn't far from here," She pointed towards the concrete jungle that was the city of Chicago. A group of homeless people swarmed to them upon leaving the park's property line. Each had a sob story worse than the person before them. They all asked for change. Some offered their Venmo in lieu of physical money if their targets claimed not to have any money on them. One woman even had a portable point of sale system that attached directly to his state of the art, iPhone fifteen. She also carried with her a large piece of cardboard with a QR code to her Cashapp, and a note that read, "I don't want food. Any donations will go directly to toward the purchase of drugs and alcohol." Death felt compelled to donate to that her. He took out Sanjeet's phone and scanned the woman's code. He transferred a hundred dollars to her as he walked by her.

"I love boys town," Death said as they crossed the street. He placed Sanjeet's phone back into his pocket. Another homeless person, this time a man, asked for changed once they crossed. He seemed angry that the last ten people had given him bags of fresh, hot food from pretty decent restaurants around the area instead of money. A moderate collection of bags containing sustenance accumulated around him on top of an old, raggedy blanket on which he was sitting. "Believe it or not, I was in that area a lot around the early eighties, and some into the nineties. It's been a long time since then," Death said. He seemed to be remembering that time fondly as a subtle smile took over his lips.

"I know, right?" Fran turned to look at Death as they walked. For almost an entire city block, a homeless woman and her dog stared as she seemingly spoke to no one while walking backwards. The woman decided not to approach Fran for a handout in fear of having to deal with a crazy person. The homeless woman then talked to her dog and waited intently for an answer. The dog wagged its tail and pissed on her leg. The homeless woman prayed for Fran, a seemingly mentally ill person, as she allowed her dog to conclude its business.

Fran walked fast through the city streets, even while walking backwards. Only tourists were foolish enough to walk slowly, or even come to a complete stop before reaching their destinations. Those who stopped either got swarmed by a group of homeless people panhandling, or trampled by busy business people trying to catch a train back to the suburbs so they could spend time with their wives, or husbands, they didn't really like but felt compelled to stay with out of a morbid loyalty to societal standards, or who were late to go to a place they really didn't want to go to only so that they could sit at a meeting they didn't want to attend because it would have been much more efficient to have just sent out an email instead. There was also the very real possibility of being stabbed by a tweaker.

"Don't make eye contact," Death said. He stiffened his neck and looked forward as they walked past a homeless vet and his girlfriend. He sat in a wheelchair, and it was obvious that he was a double amputee. His knee, or nub, peaked through the end of his army green, tattered shorts. His girlfriend sat beside him. Her back was against a light post. It appeared that she couldn't be bothered as she took pictures of herself on her phone. She held out her hands in a peace sign while doing duck lips.

"Sorry," Fran made I contact with the legless veteran. He looked at him through suffering eyes. His beard was almost long enough to reach his lap. It was in no way kept neatly. He looked like the broke version of Gandalf. The sorry was directed at the homeless man, and his girlfriend who was now pushing her breasts closer to each other so that her cleavage could show more appealing like. Fran covered her face with one hand as they continued walking.

"Please tell me we are almost there," Death pleaded. His feet were beginning to hurt from walking on the hard Chicago concrete. His voice had been negated, though, by the sound of a wailing ambulance. The noise punctured his ear drums, along with everybody else's on the same stretch of street. The sound was only amplified as it bounced from one concrete building onto another. A gust of wind swept in from the lake, causing some homeless man's cigarettes to go flying. A police car followed closely behind the ambulance, further aiding in the deafening of anyone who walked through that street. Two blocks over, a homeless man had stabbed another homeless person. Death could make out a shape of a soul from a distance as it exited the stabbed homeless person's body, but he was fairly certain that Sanjeet had fixed Andrea, the pro-union AI designed to help his workload by then.

"What is it?" Fran noticed Death becoming distracted. Three homeless people followed them, seemingly competing between one another for a handout.

"Oh, nothing. Some homeless guy got stabbed down the street, and his soul is roaming around. I'm not too worried. Sanjeet is taking care of it," Death said. He looked smug. Fran nodded as though this were something normal people normally experienced.

"Is that why the sirens ran through here, fucking everyone's ears up?" she asked. There was a soft ringing in her ear. "Don't you have to take care of that soul?"

"Like I said, I got it covered. I negotiated with my pro union soul collector, AI thing. She should be picking up the soul any moment now," Death explained.

"I didn't know AI programs had unions," Fran said.

"They don't. I'm making sure of that," Death explained. "Don't worry about it. Worry about your own soul," he continued.

"Alright," Fran shrugged her shoulders as if it weren't weird at all that Death had a personal AI program collecting souls for him. She was really living in the future. *Even Death had his own app*, she thought. She strongly considered starting one of her own. "This is it," she said as she stomped her feet in front of the second tallest building in Chicago. She rested her hands against her hips, and sighed a sigh of relief, mostly because she was tired of walking and being harassed by homeless people. Death also gave himself room to relax. He didn't have to worry about being stabbed as much anymore.

"How do you know this is the right place?" Death asked. Fran turned to talk to him. The doorman working for the building watched as she spoke at nothing. He really hoped that she wasn't about to walk into his building, or even worse, consider moving there.

"Cause the cat told me where he used to live, and the lovely gay couple at his old place in boys town said he remembered Frank mentioning his new address.

Apparently, he'd invited them over, but they didn't like his whole conman vibe," she flailed her arms as she spoke.

The door man pretended not to watch her. *This bitch is crazy*, he thought. Then he realized he didn't get paid enough to deal with crazy people, but the job paid the bills.

———————————————

Death and Fran stepped into the elevator. The thing itself was rather unassuming. There was nothing about it that struck them as anything of the ordinary. They were gold colored (not to be confused with gold plated) buttons at about waist level (depending on the height of the person standing next to it) that spanned against a shiny metallic panel up to about eye level for someone of about six feet in height. The elevator had been kept in excellent condition, despite its older appearance. Presumably, it looked the same way it had looked back in the sixties when it was installed. The most impressive thing about the elevator car was the weight limit of about thirty-three hundred pounds, despite how small it was. Realistically, it could only fit about five people comfortably, and unless you were a cast member of my six-hundred-pound life, and those around you were also part of the show, the car could easily move five people up and down all day. There was also soft jazz coming from small speakers. Death looked around to see where they sat but had no clue where ratchet sounds were coming from.

"Do you think there's a guy out there that gets called, and the person calling is like," Hey, cool cat, I need a cool, soft jazz composer, are you in?", and the guy calling wears cool sunglasses in doors because, let's face it, he's just super cool. Then the composer is like, "say no more." Then the composer forgets he doesn't actually know where to meet the caller, so he's like, "wait, where am I going, and what am I doing? Please, tell me more,"" Death rants. He looks up and down, side to side, under the carpet, over some paneling on the ceiling, but he can't find the speaker box playing the dreadful music. "Then the caller pays the composer an insane amount of money for this shit?" He waved his hands around as if Fran could see the soft jazz music all around her. If he tried, he could see the melody in the air. It was something he learned how to do after experimenting with LSD for the better part of the nineteen sixties. He was one of those hippies that liked to do drugs, and sing at bonfires, however he was pro Vietnam war since he was all about collecting souls. He really wished Fran could see certain types of music. This, however, nightmarish, soft elevator jazz was nothing he wished for even his most hated enemy. If his ears could bleed, they would have created vast pools of blood the moment the music touched them.

"Also, the guy tells the composer, "The music has to be dreadfully boring,""

Death nodded in agreement. "And annoying as hell," he added.

Fran wondered, allowing her thoughts to become worthy of being shower thoughts. She fought the urge to press all hundred plus buttons on the shiny panel. Death's issue with elevator music was now simply an afterthought. She didn't particularly like elevator music herself, but the shiny buttons took precedence over her ability to pay attention. Both her and Death stared awkwardly into an empty hallway as the elevator stopped at a random floor. They poked their heads out of the car and saw that there was no one running toward the elevator. They moved their heads back into the car and pushed the close door button.

Death tapped his thigh with his hand repeatedly. Fran looked at her phone, then checked her email, exited the screen, then checked her email once more and scrolled through old messages. She never actually had a reason to check her email. She wasn't like those fancy people with office jobs that had to dread waiting for the one email that could change the company. Most of her correspondence consisted of spam and junk mail, and African prince's claiming to have riches waiting for her. She always wanted to see what happened if she replied to one of those African royalties. Maybe they weren't full of shit, and she was passing up on an opportunity of a lifetime. She could see herself as an African queen, with her nearly transparent pale skin. She would make sure that the money and fame wouldn't get to her head. She'd be a humble queen. A queen of the people.

"Are these things always so slow?" Death asked. Fran turned to answer as the door closed shut. The car jolted harshly as it restarted its trek toward the highest floor, very, very slowly. In the grand scheme of things, what was a few mind-numbing minutes when it came to Fran regaining possession of her soul. This was something she just had to deal with, especially since she was the one that put herself in that situation to start with. Death, on the other hand, couldn't wait to get out of the confines of the elevator. For Death, between the closing of the elevator doors twice (now for the second time. The first time when they first entered the car. The second when the doors opened on their own for no reason), and how long it took for the car to move from the bottom floor, the wait was nearly equivalent to a lifetime of suffering. God forbid there were strangers on board, sharing the car with them. Then, the time it took to get to their destination would have been amplified to feel like, at the very least, two entire lifetimes.

"To tell you the truth," Fran said. She put her phone down for the sixteenth time. "I don't normally get on these things. I never have a reason to," she said. Now that the car was moving at a steady pace, they could make out the faint sounds of elevator music in the background again. Death bobbed his head nervously. He didn't quite know why he felt so nervous. It was certainly not due to being alone with Fran in a tight, enclosed space, where he couldn't just walk away from her if she suddenly became too boring, or annoying. There were plenty of times they'd been together alone, in similarly small spaces, like when she tries on different outfits at department stores. In some instances, they'd even seen each other naked, and they didn't feel as awkward as they do now, as they rode up a strange elevator. Beside when she'd ask for his advice while trying on new clothing, Death had a horrible tendency to blast screamo music on his headphones, and open the bathroom door without knocking, which caused him to walk in on Fran, fully naked, as she was taking a shower on more than one occasion. Yes, things were awkward, and strained for the remainder of the day, but never did they feel awkward being around one another after.

The first time was a little uncomfortable, but then they both realized there was no sexual tension, or creepiness between them. She didn't really care if he saw her nude. He was more like a gay best friend. She had nothing to worry about. Even Fran had seen him naked on several different instances. Once, when he spilled red wine on his robe. He hadn't packed a day bag, and he certainly wasn't about to leave Fran's house with a stain on his clothes, so, without much of a warning, he undressed in her laundry room and hung out in there, butt naked, while his clothes washed and dried. Thanks to his lack of communication, Fran walked into her laundry room after hearing her washer going, when she vividly remembered herself turning the machine off. Also, laundry day wasn't for another day or two, so there was no reason for the machine to be on as it was. So, she opened the laundry room door without as much a care in the world, because she was in her own apartment, and caught Death cat walking naked. He was performing a fashion show for a congregation of imagined cameras, and fashion enthusiasts. He quickly attempted to cover his private parts, but then remembered he had none.

"What? You've never seen a naked skeleton pretending to be on a fashion runway before?" he said to her head as she was peaking in. The rest of her body stood behind the other side of the door.

"I'm. I don't-" Fran had been left without words, but that was certainly not the last time they would see each other in their birthday suits.

So why, then, was it mind bogglingly awkward to stand next to one another in a small elevator while fully clothed? Death looked up. He caught her eye. She bobbed her head up and down. Then he looked back at the floor. Fran locked her hands in front of her. The elevator music surrounding their auditory senses served as an unintended tool that slowed time as they knew it. Fran played with her hair. She tucked a strand of it behind her ear. She soon looked away upon making eye contact. She looked up at the buttoned panel. They weren't even halfway up the building. The air inside their confined, shared space began to feel stuffy, and stale. It was as though the oxygen inside it was running out. If Death could sweat, his armpits would have been flooded by now.

"How many floors are there?" Fran asked. She pulled on her V-neck collar. Every now and again, she liked to flaunt her femineity by showing a little skin. Her boobs, however, did not fill out her shirt as much as she would have liked them to. She felt cursed for being as petite as she was.

"Yeah. Does this thing just have one speed? Snail?" Death snickered. His question was a rhetorical one. They both let out a nervous laugh.

Death couldn't understand how things were only getting weirder, and more uncomfortable. His stomach rumbled, but not in the way it does when one experiences hunger. He'd eaten Mexican food shortly before meeting with Fran at the bean, and he was about to pay the price. He took a step and a half away from Fran. Albeit it was a short step and a half on account of them being in an ultra-small space to begin with. He fought the urge to fart, but he couldn't contain himself. His stomach was hurting too much to maintain any level of manners. Silently, he released his first toot like a ninja. It was a small one. He could begin to feel the pain in his stomach dissipate, if only a little. With any luck, the fart would be the non-smelly type. He waited to see if there was any reaction from Fran. There was none that he could see. Even if she'd smelled it, he was rather confident that he could chalk the smell up to faulty piping on whatever floor they were passing. After all, the building was old, and the pipes were most likely corroded. His stomach, though, continued suffering. He weighed his options. His first fart had been successfully executed without a hitch. Surely, if he tried, the second, and hopefully last, fart would be as successful.

The rumbles in his stomach intensified. He was beginning to get stomach cramps, and his sphincter was having trouble containing his gas. Death felt several large fart bubbles moving about in his stomach. His brow began to sweat. He took a look at Fran, who wondered why the service on her phone wasn't working. Death clenched his butt cheeks, horrified that the next fart to escape his body would not be as forgiving as the first. His lower stomach ached. He could notice it becoming distended as it did when he fought the first fart. Death was fighting the fight of his life against a fart. He turned his gaze toward the button panel. Twenty floors to go. The formerly dreaded swanky tunes were now no more than randomly assorted noises in the background.

With his stomach about to blow, and the elevator moving as slow as it was, Death had no choice but to try and let his God forsaken gasses leak out of him discreetly. Fran looked at him. She smiled awkwardly. Death looked at the ceiling. He closed his eyes and prayed like he'd never prayed before. He let the fate of his butt cheeks up to the discretion of a higher power.

At first, Fran could hear the faintest of long, high-pitched sounds that bordered the pitch at which one would use to attract a group of rabid dogs, and that of which could barely be perceived by the human ear. It like was a shy trumpet. The faint sound grew louder, and with it, Death's face slowly turned beat red. Before long, his fart was at its loudest, with no signs of reprieved. The smell followed soon after. Fran initially attempted to ignore the continuous butt trumpet, but ultimately burst into laughter, then terror as the smell hit her olfactory senses. She grabbed her throat as though she were choking. The veins on her neck distended as she tried not to inhale the toxic fart. The smell burned the nerve endings on her nose. The burning feeling, though, did nothing to mask the smell that was escaping Death's third eye.

"Oh my god, dude, are you dying?" Fran could barely utter a word. Her face turned green. She gasped as though she were dying. She frantically pressed the button for the floor they were headed to as if it would help the elevator go any faster.

Death stood stiller than her though could be still. Maybe if he didn't move, Fran wouldn't be able to tell he was still there. Finaly, the elevator dinged, indicating they'd arrived at their destination. Fran exited the elevator so quickly that she fell upon exiting. She gulped big breaths of non-farted air. Her neck veins returned to normal as the freshly cycled oxygen hit her lungs. Remnants of the fart escaped the elevator, but thankfully it was diluted by the air in the hallway. The hallway itself had several different aromas of mouthwatering food.

———————————

"This is it," Fran and Death approached Frank's door. Death looked skeptical, but he knew he had no room to question Fran's instincts after having nearly killed her with his fart but did so anyway.

"Are you sure?" Death asked. He chose to ignore what had just happened. He really hoped Fran would forget about the whole thing.

"It's our best lead," she sighed.

"What are you going to do with all that money from the loan once you get your soul back?" Death asked. "Assuming everything goes well, and Frank plays nice," he added.

"My first thought was to get a new apartment. Then, maybe invest in some real-estate. I have to make that money back somehow if I don't want to be screwed when I die," she said.

"I'm not sure that it's a good market for that right now," Death said. He had no clue what he was talking about.

"Why not?" she asked.

"Something about rates going up," he said. He'd heard that on the news one time. He had barely paid attention to what the news anchor was saying. He just felt sophisticated, being able to say something about the housing market.

"You make a good point," she said. Death agreed. "Even if it were a good market, the whole dying before I repay the loan thing freaks me out," she added. The walk from the elevator to Frank's door was not far. They walked up to the only red door in the hallway. He must have either replaced it, or painted it over as soon as he moved in. An impressive feat, considering how crazy the building bi laws that governed its residents was about any type of renovations. Fran knocked on the red door three solid times. "I feel like one of those cops. Open up, it's the police," she whispered in between a giggle. Death took a few steps back and pretended to kick the door down.

"Do you think I could knock this down if I tried?" he asked her.

"Maybe. We should try it one day," she said. Death puffed out his chest. He stood the way he imagined a cop would stand when on a quest to apprehend a bad guy.

Death reverted back to the investing conversation. "Yeah, it's one of those risks, though. If you can pull it off, you could make a good little empire for yourself. You just have to be smart," he said. He knew that telling her about her life expectancy was against the rules, but he tried to allude to it without actually revealing her expiration date. "You might live to be a hundred and twenty-three years. That's plenty of time to pay off a debt." He felt very proud of himself.

"That's a very specific number," she said.

"It was a totally random number that I completely pulled out of nothing. Don't look too much into it," he told her. Her actual life expectancy was to be a hundred and twenty-four years. A whole year more than what he alluded to, so technically he didn't break any rules. It wasn't as if he hinted at that number being anywhere near what it actually was. As far as he knew, he was in the clear in terms of the rules in his Grim Reaper handbook, which also happened to be the most important rule in the book. Would he have truly revealed the date at which she'd die, he would have been smitten by God's dads lightning bolts by now.

"I don't care about a fucking extended car warranty!" a muffled, angry voice shouted from the other side of the red door.

"Frank?" Fran asked. She leaned her ear against the cold red door and knocked again. Death hovered over her, putting his ear against the door as well.

"I don't think knocking again will make him open the door any sooner," Death said. She looked up at him and rolled her eyes.

"Who's asking?" the muffled voice asked from the other side. Presumably, it was Frank.

It's Fran, the girl from your tent. Before the whole place got shut down!" she reminded him, unintentionally reopening a healing wound.

"I wouldn't bring things up that would piss him off," Death said.

"Shut up. I don't work well under pressure," she said.

"Oh yeah. Did you ever find out what happened to that place?" Death asked. His face was still firmly planted against the door. He used both his hands to keep pressure off his neck. She looked at him with inquisitive eyes.

"I didn't tell you?"

"No. Remember? I had to leave, and we've been fighting through homeless people the entire way here," he said.

"Dude, you were right there when Catgatha was telling us. Now I remember." She moved away from the red door. He followed. Death crossed his arms as if in thought. He looked up.

"I was in the middle of an important call with God," he said.

"From what I remember, you were too busy with the realization that there were more of you. I recall you being excited about unicorns," she said. "I'm pretty sure that was the first time you'd even looked at your Grim Reaper Handbook.

"Was not."

"Whatever," she disregarded him. "You were so distracted.

Death was about to make his rebuttal but was rudely interrupted by the clinking sounds of Frank's door locks popping and clicking open. He cracked his door just enough for Death and Fran to see a sliver of his face. "What are you doing here, Richard? Oh, hey little girl. I remember you," Frank said. He felt a ball in his throat when he saw her.

"Ha! Little girl," Death laughed. He held his stomach.

"Shut up," Fran pouted. "I'm not little. I'm just fun sized," she said. She crossed her arms and stomped twice. Her face was pouty.

"You're not helping your case," Frank said.

"He's right," Death added.

"Shut up. Also, how does he know you, Dick?" she poked at Death.

"She can see you?" Frank asked.

"Yeah," Death sighed. She won't leave me alone."

"Excuse me, you're the one following me like a puppy," Fran said. She stood up straight, trying to make herself appear more menacing. Frank looked at her with a blank face.

"Checks out. He's so needy," Frank said. "What do you want?" he asked.

"Fran, in case you weren't aware, Frank is a demon," Death mansplained.

"A what?" Fran asked. "I thought demons were cute little black cats." She sounded thoroughly surprised.

"That's racist," Death said. "Demons, just like grim reapers as I recently learned, can come in all shapes and sizes. Don't generalize, you jerk." Death was offended at her racism.

"Leave the poor girl alone, man. How was she supposed to know," Frank interjected.

Fran felt validated by her soul's captor. "I'm starting to like this guy a little more than you, Dick," she teased. Why'd you wait so long to tell me Frank was a demon?" she asked.

"You never asked," Death said. "Besides, how was I supposed to know your Frank was my Frank?"

"Aren't you like all knowing?" she asked. Frank stared at them from behind his barely cracked open door. A small metal chain prevented it from opening up any further.

"No? you're thinking about God," Death said. Frank nodded.

"But you're a celestial, or something."

"You forget. I'm more or less a gig worker. I'm like an uber, but different. Instead of giving rides, or delivering fatty food, I deliver souls. I'm still a contractor, but one who works on an assignment basis and deals with dead people. I don't know shit about what anyone is doing," Death explained.

"I'll let you two work things out," Frank said. Fran wedged her foot between the door and the door frame, preventing Frank from shutting it closed. Death then used his weight to push it open, but realized the chain door that would prevent him from busting it open. Frank sighed. "For God's sake. Fine. Let me close the door so I can remove the chain," he said.

Frank removed the door. Death became impatient. "I'm going to tear the door down," he told Fran.

"Relax, dude. He said he'd get it open."

"Do you really trust the guy that conned you out of your soul?" he asked. Death rolled up his sleeves. He slapped his face in an effort to hype himself up. "Stand back, Fran. This might get ugly," he said. He shoved her aside, then moved as far back as he could before hitting the other side of the wall. "One," he counted. "Two," he prepared his leg to kick open the door. "Three!" Death placed his entire weight behind his kicking leg. Frank opened the door moments before Death's foot met the door, causing Death to fall forward into Frank's apartment. Death landed in a split. He let out a painful sounding yelp as Fran walked slowly past him into Franks living room.

Frank and Fran walked towards his sleek modern couch. "I love the coffee table," she said.

"It came with the place. I'm still deciding on if I want to keep it," he said.

Death stood up slowly. He held his crotch once he was on his feet. Fran laughed at him silently as she took a seat. "I'm so sorry about him," she said. Death flicked his wrist, causing a stack of magazine to fall violently off of Frank's coffee table. Frank pinched the bridge of his nose as he took a deep breath. He promised himself that he wasn't going to let other people trigger his anger issues. It dawned on Fran that their host was standing by the window in only his underwear. The same underwear that had a hole on it that revealed his hairy butt cheek, and the one the delivery guy had the displeasure of seeing.

"If you're back here for your soul, I don't got it anymore," Frank said. He looked at Death as he tried to save face and pretended that he hadn't just crushed his family jewels while attempting to break an entering. He made his best attempt at brushing the incident off. As though nothing happened. Fran also looked at Death. She couldn't decide if she should feel bad for him or not. Ultimately, she decided that Death had done it to himself, so she moved on.

"How? I don't understand?" she asked Frank. Frank closed the door, then walked to the kitchen. His adonis body laid in full display. She could tell he wasn't human based on the excessive amount of hair on his shoulders, and back, and basically all over his body. Then she remembered that he's a demon, so it made sense. In the gay community, he was considered a rather sexy bear. An invasive thought then became jealous as she realized how the extra hair could help, practically speaking, during the colder months in Chicago. Having an extra layer of insulation could always be helpful when it was zero degrees outside, and the air hurt her face. She could always choose to shave her body during the warmer season.

"You really think I was just going to keep your soul for safe keeping?" Frank asked. He reached for a cup of coffee. "I'm sending you an invoice for the magazines you destroyed," he pointed at Death.

"Death looked side to side, and behind him. "Me?" he pointed at himself.

"Yeah, for the magazines you messed up," Frank accused him.

"Didn't you just get ten million dollars for Fran's soul?" Death's words punched Fran right in the gut. She shot him a look that indicated she was hurt. The way that said, *please, don't remind me. I can never forget myself for this.*

"Ten million dollars," Frank dropped a full cup of hot coffee at the sound of ten million dollars. Fran nodded sadly.

Death walked closer to the kitchen. "You sound surprised," he said.

"That son of a bitch!" Frank shouted. He pulled at his already messy hair.

"Sounds like someone conned the conman," Fran grinned.

"Sure does," Death followed.

"There's no way. No way her soul is worth that much," Frank said. He was on the verge of hyperventilating.

"It was actually worth more before she gave it away. That cost her at least a couple million," Death rubbed insult to injury.

"Holy shit, really?" ask. She was in disbelief. Death raised both of his arms to his side and showed them his palms as he shrugged.

"How much did he give you?" Death asked.

"He? Who's he?" Fran asked.

"The fucken Devil," Frank shouted at no one specifically. He was in shock from what was developing in front of him. "Five hundred K," he whispered. He took a step, forgetting the hot coffee that had pool below him after hearing about how much money he'd lost. Frank let out a loud yelp, and awkwardly hopped out of the kitchen.

"Is it too late for you to call and ask for it back?" Fran asked.

"Yeah, let me give him a call and ask really nicely," Frank said sarcastically.

"You would do that for me?" Frank looked at her as she had some type of cognitive disability he didn't know about that made it difficult for her to understand sarcasm. If she did, she'd been hiding it very well until that point.

"Are you kidding me?" Frank looked at Death. "This girl," he added. "I can't just call him and ask for your soul back, sweety. The deal is done. He gave me the money, and I sent him the paperwork you signed," he explained.

"I did that under duress. You had me distracted by promises of ghosts, and old timey witches. Oh, and my chair ghost," she said excitedly.

"Not my problem, toots."

"Charles? Died of a heart attack on your chair Charles? He was a great guy. Had a weird obsession with that chair of your in life, and, as it seems, in Death. He won't leave it. That's literally what's been keeping me from collecting him," Death said. He zoned in on Frank's mail and began to open it. Frank punched him and took his mail back.

"Listen. I'm going to be nice to you, but only because I was ripped off myself." Frank god closer to Fran. He leaned closer to her ears. So close that she could feel the heat from his face against her earlobe. "If you want your soul back, you're going to have to go pay a visit to the Devil himself," Frank whispered. Death stole an apple from a fruit tray on Frank's dining table. He took a bite, but quickly regretted it. He spit it out once he realized it was made of wax.

Fran wrapped her arms around herself. "Does that mean what I think it means?" she asked. Death placed the bitten wax apple back on the fruit tray. He did his best to pretend nothing happened.

"You're going to hell," Frank said.

"Hey! What did I do?" Fran asked defensively. "Oh," she said after realizing she'd literally have to go down to the depths of hell. "Is it really a fiery hellscape like everyone says it is?" she asked. Her face was inquisitive.

Frank picked at his ears. He took a wad of ear wax out, inspected it, then flicked it across the room. "The whole idea that there's fire everywhere is absurd," he said. Fran could tell this was a sore subject for him. "It pisses me off that one nut had a bad trip, and all of a sudden hell gets a bad rap. We actually really care about our environment, unlike you dumb humans. The devil makes sure we keep only the bests of the best on his environmental payroll." Fran adjusted her feet on the couch and sat with her legs crossed. She grabbed one of his couch cushions and cuddled with it. "Please, were you raised by wolves? Take a seat like a normal person. You animal." He asked.

"So sorry," she said, and sat back down with her feet on the ground. She was a lot less comfortable now.

"Don't worry about it. At least you're not like this guy." He points at Death as he wonders how to peel a wax banana. "None of those are edible, you genius!" he shouted.

"I knew that," Death mumbled. He waited a moment for Frank to divert his attention back to Fran. Then he placed the wax banana into one of his pockets for later inspection.

"If you ask me, hell is more like a utopia in every manner of speaking," he explained. He moved his hands vividly like the Italians do when they explain things.

"Then what's so bad about it?" Fran asked. Frank made his way around the couch and sat across from her on his coffee table. His stomach formed several rolls of skin covered, sheep hair looking hair. She cringed as he sat with his legs spread apart.

"People tend to live out some of their worst fears," he said, unbothered by both the obvious sign of disgust Fran had on her face. He leaned closer. His stomach prevented him from leaning too far, though. "Like being forced to pay full price at thrift shops, or having no choice but than to answer your mom's phone calls and having to explain to her why you're still single level fears." Her face reddened. Seriously. Does she not know how crappy the dating pool is? It's all dick pics and gluten allergies," Frank ranted. "Although," he switched gears. "A nice dick pic never hurt anyone. Unless that dick belonged to a prong dicked jelly fish. Let me tell you. I don't recommend doing it with a jelly fish. I tell you this from experience, girl. No one ever told me not to. Then, thirty-eight stitches on my taint later…" Death overheard, and he grabbed his butt as he imagined the pain.

"It sounds horrible," was all Fran could say.

"Just think of your worst nightmare, and that's what the Devil will use against you for an eternity," he cemented his point in her head.

Fran's body shook involuntarily on his couch. "So how do we get to hell?" she asked.

"This view is amazing," Death said as he stared out the window.

"I know, right?" Frank said. "Rent ain't too bad, neither."

"Focus! You two," Fran shouted. "Death, you're killing me," she accused him.

"I'm just standing here," he said.

"Getting there is easy," Frank told her. She leaned in. "Managing to get an audience with the Devil is the hard part. It's even harder to get out alive," he continued.

"Why?" She seemed confused.

"You ever heard of Dante's Inferno?" Frank asked. She nodded. Her eyes were as wide as half dollars. Death broke his attention from the view. He sat next to Fran and nodded as well. "Well, he decided to pull Dante's nine levels of hell because HR thought that this new generation of souls were too weak. They kept breaking. He got no use for broken souls. So, HR implemented a version of his inferno that was both eternally terrifying, yet vanilla enough not to break souls too quickly," Frank complained. "Now they got this new guy called Roberto."

"So, Dante just left?"

"He didn't so much as leave as the Devil let him go. Lucy was all for him. It was HR that had the problem. He was also too expensive, so we got Roberto and his four levels of moderate to severe inconvenience. Whoever wants an audience with Lucy has to prove that they're worthy enough to be in his presence by clearing all of Roberto's challenges."

"I'm going to miss Dante," Death said. I remember he invited me to a party. I didn't realize it was his going away party."

"Sucks to suck. It was great," Frank said. I miss him too though. That guy knew how to throw a great party. He was also a really good listener. Do you remember when the Devil's wife left him? Dante was the only one who could tolerate the guy's never-ending wailing."

"I remember that," Death said.

"I still don't know how the guy did it. Freaking lucy cried for millenniums."

"Why'd she leave him again?" Death asked.

"Yeah? What happened?" Fran wondered out loud.

"The bitch met someone," Frank said.

Death placed a hand on his chin and nodded. "Do you know where he went?" he asked.

"Lucy?"

"No, Dante," Death said.

"Last I heard he was in the Bahamas, taking advantage of his fat severance package with his wife, Doreen."

"Guys!" Fran circled back to her issue. Both Frank and Death tensed up and got back on track.

"As I was saying. Roberto's got these four levels. Don't ask me what they are. I haven't had a chance to check them out yet. They constantly change, too, so no one really knows what to expect."

"Okay, how do we get there?" She asked.

"You ready to go now?"

"I guess. She rested her chin on her hands.

"Wait, we? Not we, you!" Death panicked.

"Frank stood up. "This might hurt a little bit." Without warning, he clocked both Death and Fran square in the face while chanting something that resembled Latin.

Roberto's Moderate to Severe Inconveniences.

Chapter 9:

Fran grunted. Death let out a loud snore. Drool oozed from his mouth as his body lay bent in half, like a really stretchy scorpion. Fran opened her eyes slowly, having to blink rapidly several times as her pupils adjusted to the bright fluorescent lights that shined from above. The first thing she noticed was that she was lying next to Death's discombobulated skeleton. His right leg was five feet to the north of the small, sterile office. His torso rested above his head while his right arm hung from a coat rack near what must have been the entrance door.

"I'll have to call you later, Lucy. I think you got some visitors," Priscilla said from behind her desk. She had a nasal sounding voice, but she refused to visit her ENT because she knew he'd force her to get surgery in order to fix her deviated septum. A large computer monitor hid her face from Fran and Death.

"Have they gone through Roberto's moderate to severe inconveniences yet?" The Devil asked.

"Are you sure we can't bring Dante back? He was such a nice guy," Priscilla asked. He sounded whiny. Meanwhile Fran picked up Death's body parts and began to help him reassemble.

"Can we just drop the whole Dante thing? I'm sure HR has their reasons for letting him go. They know what they are doing," The Devil said. He was tired of having to explain to the rest of the company why their most beloved torturer was no longer with them. She could tell from the sound of his voice that Dante's departure was still a fresh wound. "Besides, corporate is all about affirmative action. Roberto is just a way they are trying to adhere to these new stupid policies."

Priscilla pressed the issue no further. "I'll have these guys go through Roberto's hellish challenge then, sir." She hung up the phone. Her face rested in perpetual state of not giving any fucks. Others would call it bitch face, but the vocabulary hadn't made its way down to hell yet. "Welcome, you two," she said with approximately zero enthusiasm in her voice. Fran slapped Death's face around until he woke up.

Death jerked awake. He jumped to his feet in a defensive ninja stance. "Where the hell are we?"

"Bingo," Priscilla said. "Sort of." Death relaxed. Fran walked up to Priscilla's desk. "This is hell's waiting room for those who aren't quite dead yet. Do you have an appointment? If not, go away. I'm busy."

"We've come to talk to the Devil." Fran said confidently.

"Yeah, okay, but do you have an appointment?" Priscilla asked once more. Her voice grew impatient.

"Well, no," Fran said. She turned to Death.

"Don't look at me," he said.

"Please!" she brandished a pair of irresistible puppy eyes.

Death squirmed for a moment. "Okay, fine. Just tell him she's with me," he told Priscilla.

"It doesn't work that way, sweetheart," she said just before blowing an enormous pink bubble gum bubble. It popped once it got too big, causing Death to jump slightly. Priscilla opened a drawer under her desk and reached for a nail file.

"Do you know who I am?" Death asked. He puffed his chest.

"Don't know. Don't care. Don't make me call security, asshole," she said. The unimpressed secretary began to file her long pointy nails into an even pointier point.

"Excuse my, uh, friend," Fran said. "He's a little special," she pantomimed.

Priscilla looked up with only her eyeballs and grinned a very subtle grin. She continued filing her fingernails. She was very careful not to ruin her light pink nail polish. "Take a number sweety. Then go take a seat. I'll call you when your number is up." A ticket with the number six, six, six materialized on Priscilla's desk. It smoked for a moment as it cooled off from having shown up out of thin air.

Fran cautiously patted the ticket. "What's this for?" she asked once she was certain the ticket was cool enough to touch. She picked up it and observed it. The numbers were in an old English type of font. There was a watermark behind the numbers. It was a picture of what humans thought the Devil looked like. It was a goat with long horns, standing on its hind feet, holding a chalice upright with one hand. On the other hand, he held a naked woman close to his body. The goat looking Devil looked down toward the naked woman in a way that said he was most likely going to fuck her up both sexually, and physically.

"It's your ticket. That's how you'll know it's your turn to go through that door and start Roberto's challenges."

"Tell me again why I have to go through those challenges?" Fran asked Priscilla sighed angrily.

"To earn an audience with the Devil, sweetheart. Now please take a seat and wait for your number to be called." Pricilla pointed at a suede, burgundy loveseat across from her desk, next to the door. Fran and Death looked around to see if there were any other visitors, but, besides themselves, and Priscilla, they were the only occupants.

The loveseat was just big enough to seat the both of them. Death and Fran had to wiggle their way onto the seat. Their thighs pressed tightly against each other.

"Can you scooch just a little?" Fran asked. She grunted as she attempted to make herself comfortable. "Your boney leg is hurting me." She shifted. Death crossed one leg over the other. He moved his weight onto one butt cheek in an effort to make space for her. As he did this, he accidentally dug his elbow on the side of her stomach. Fran fought a yelp from escaping her mouth, but ultimately ended sounding like a mouse who'd just been stepped on. "For fuck's sake, I'll just stand," she said and stood up.

"Please remain seated!" Priscilla yelled without taking her eyes off her monitor.

Death readjusted as Fran begrudgingly took her uncomfortable seat back. "Is this part of the challenge?" she whispered to Death.

"One would think," he said.

They origamied their body for over an hour. Finally, they'd come to a position that both found bearable. For a moment, the room fell quiet. The stillness of it all sank in. It was as though time itself was too afraid to bother Priscilla as she performed her secretarial duties, which, as it seemed, consisted of intermittently complaining about not getting paid enough to take care of two bozos that came in uninvited. Presumably that was the only thing she'd done in a very long time, considering her phone had rung approximately zero times during Fran's and Death's entire visit, they were fairly certain she didn't do much at all.

Fran tapped her fingers against the loveseat's upholstery. She considered asking the secretary for an estimate, but decided it was most likely not a good idea.

"My bones are starting to fuse together," Death joked.

"Shh!" Priscilla shushed sharply. "Six, six, six!" she shouted shortly after. She waved the duo over to her desk. Death struggle to stand up. So did Fran. He limped his way over to the desk. Fran felt as though her hip was detaching as she walked. Her hip joints shouted with loud, painful pops. She waddled the rest of the short way to the desk.

You're such an old man," Fran told him.

"And you're not so nimble yourself. You're waddling like a nine-month pregnant lady," he shot back.

"Here's the deal," Priscilla handed each of them a thick stack of paperwork. The legal documents were still warm from having come out of the printer. Priscilla adjusted her cat eye shaped reading glasses snuggle against the bridge of her nose. Her breath smelled of a perpetual amount of coffee, and it made its way up to Fran and Death's nostrils. Death could tell the woman liked a good blonde roast from the smell of it. "I'm going to need you

two to sign some waivers, and photo releases, and stuff of
that nature." She licked her index finger and flipped
through every page, pointing at the parts that needed their
signatures, and highlighting them with bright pink
highlighter.

"Seems like a lot," Fran hesitated. She looked at
Death for any sign indicating she should wait, but he was
finishing off the last of his signatures. "You're missing an
initial here," Priscilla instructed him. Something deep
within Fran screamed at her not to sign.

"Are you just going to stand there and look pretty?"
the secretary hissed. Fran became bug eyes and fearful.
"No, really. You look beautiful! What type of moisturizer
do you use?"

Fran arched an eyebrow. Generic store brand?" she
signed the paperwork despite her gut feeling. Priscilla
opened a loud metal drawer and plopped the stack of each
of their paperwork into it. A loud thunk rattled the room,
sending a thick cloud of dust flying from below her desk.
She waved it off, then took a moment to wipe off her
glasses.

"Here's the deal. There are four challenges. Each
challenge will be even harder than the last." Death leaned

over priscilla's desk to take a closer look into the drawer. Fran also wondered what else was inside of it. "You guys listening? Eyes up here." Fran and Death shot back up to attention.

"What are the challenges?" Fran asked. Her body was stiff.

"I can only let you know of one challenge at a time."

"Because?" Fran asked. Death played with a stack of red post it notes on the desk. Priscilla smacked his hand, and Death dropped the sticky notes.

"Because if you know what the next challenge is well before you go through it, you'll have enough time to formulate a working strategy. Also, because I said so." Priscilla had no time to sugarcoat things.

"What's the first challenge?" Fran sked. Death counted the ceiling tiles.

"If you'd stop talking and asking so many questions, I'd get to that faster," Priscilla said impatiently. Fran pretended to zip her lips. "Throw it away!" Priscilla said about the imaginary key. Fran shrugged in confusion, then realized what she'd meant. With a flick of her wrist, she pretended to throw the key away. Death was hit in the eye by an invisible object. Fran chalked it up to pure coincidence, or dust from the ceiling he kept staring at.

"The first challenge is the easiest. Most easy? You will go into the room," she pointed to a rusty, bloody metal door behind them that hadn't been there when they regained their consciousness. The sheer appearance made shivers run down their spine. "Behind that door is a room. In that room there are two chairs. All you have to do is make it ten minutes in the room without going crazy. If you fail the challenge, you'll get stuck in there for the rest of eternity." She warned.

"That sounds too easy," Death said. "Good luck!" he told Fran and laughed. He started to go toward the loveseat, which now seemed cozy, knowing he didn't have to share it with Fran.

"Hey!" she yelled.

"You're going in there too, pretty boy," Priscilla pointed at her drawer.

"But I'm just tagging along!" he said. Fran burst into laughter.

"Come on, you big baby. It's just ten minutes. How hare can it be?" she said.

"I know, but this is your thing. Not mine," Death argued.

"You signed the paperwork. Now go in there before I call security and have them shove you in there," Priscilla threatened. She placed her hand over a big red button that was labeled with big white letters that said security. Death moped but turned toward the door. "I forgot to mention a tiny thing. You guys will have to listen to the best elevator music hits while you're in the room!"

247

Elevator Music.

Chapter 10:

Death and Fran took a seat. They each were given an old, rickety folding chair that was designed in a way that would prevent any bums from ever becoming too comfortable and claiming ownership of the chair. Who ever imagined it made it a goal to make the chair's lumbar region cause its user to feel as though they were developing large bulging discs in series that ran from the low back, up to the mid region. In addition, neither of the chairs were made with any symmetry in mind, which left them completely, and utterly, unleveled, and there was no trace of a wedge to help them solve the case of the wobbly chairs.

The blood metal door behind them shut closed. Each of its hinges cried in unison. It was a cacophony of sad metallic cries as it swiveled on its hinges. The sound was loud enough to make a person's ears bleed, which was almost the case for Fran. She tried her best to cover her ears. The door's shrieks lingered, or so Fran thought. Perhaps she was experiencing a severe degree of tinnitus, but it made no difference. Regardless, the echoes gingerly fell upon their final resting place, when an army of flood lights accosted Fran's and Death's optical nerves. They did their best to shield their eyes, but the light burned through Death's robe, and Fran's eyelids.

"Do you hear that?" Fran asked. Death shook his head, almost as imperceptibly as the origin of the soft tones Fran was beginning to pick up on. "It's music. Do you not hear that?" Fran opened her eyes cautiously. A vast, white room with seemingly no end, and no beginning, surrounded them. "Where are we?" She asked. The music gradually grew louder.

Death peaked his eyes open. Pain seared where his optic nerves would have been. He blinked fast as his eyesight pulled focus. For a moment, he thought there was something wrong with his vision, but later accepted that they were in a desolate void. He shrugged. That wasn't the first time he'd found himself disoriented in an odd place. His college years were wild.

"You're so helpful," Fran said.

"There! I hear it!" Death yelled. His lower back was now beginning to feel a nagging, burning ache.

"Oh, no!" Fran wavered. A pressing, tense pressure built up insider of her.

"What?" Death asked.

"Elevator music!" Upon this realization, Fran's face began to feel loose. She turned to Death. "I'm scared," she said. A tear ran down her face. She reached for Death's hand. It melted slowly between her fingers. His robe disintegrated into a million tiny spiders. "What's happening?" she asked, but he was gone. She held an oozy remnant of his arm with her hand, which was now bubbling. Portions of her face bubbled as well. It melted like high grade quesadilla cheese. Her subconscious then shattered into an infinitesimal number of tiny pieces. They witnessed her skin melted and peeled off slowly off of her skeleton while smooth jazz played in the background.

Her skeleton became porous, even more so than what a normal skeleton would be. Then, every infinite little piece of her subconscious exploded into even smaller pieces as the elevator music neared a symphonic climax. Pieces of her were now in ever conceivable existence. She was now aware of the existence of infinite dimensions, all of which now had little pieces of her. They roamed the stars, the empty void nears, and past the outer skirts of the universe, and infinity itself. They burned as they entered alien landscapes. Some of her witnessed her biggest failures in infinite realities. Other shards of her experienced her biggest fears, her regrets, rejections, and sorrows. She witnessed it all. An infinite amount of her lifetimes, from birth to death. Some deaths were more gruesome than others. Her awareness shattered and put itself back together within an ever-higher number of infinite infinities as it was for to listen to one elevator song after another. She could feel her infinite sanities losing their minds and scratching in between each brain fold for an ounce of reprieve from what was most likely the Devil's music.

Fran withered into her chair, convulsing as she scratched large swaths of skin off of her as the elevator music, and its chaotic, incomprehensible, unpredictable tones pierced her every corner of imaginable existence.

She wished she could die. Never mind reclaiming her soul. The price she had to pay as a result of selling her soul in the form of an eternity of having to answer her mom's calls seemed like child's play compared to the suffering her shattered subconscious was being forced to endure.

"Time's up." Priscilla's voice brought them back to reality. Death's eyes were now on his chin, and his mouth was where his forehead, for but a brief moment until he regained his composure. Fran still sat in her chair from hell. She rocked back and forth with both hands on her head. Heeps of sweat soaked her shirt. Her hair rested in disarray. Priscilla looked at her watch impatiently. She tapped her foot against the ground.

Fort minutes later, Fran's heart rate returned to normal. Her breathing slowed down to about twenty breaths per minute, compared to the hundred and seven breaths a minute she was taking in while in the room.

Death struggled to reconfigure his face. For him, the terror continued to some extent, until Fran placed a warm hand on his shoulder. "Come on, you big baby," she said. Death looked at her.

"But why do I have to wear leech shoes!" he asked her as they exited the chamber's threshold.

"Come on," she helped him out.

"There's a water cooler by the window. Take as much time as you need, then come back when you're ready for Roberto's next challenge." Priscilla's voice sounded almost sympathetic. She must have understood what they'd experienced.

Fran walked up to the water cooler. She pulled the curtain aside to catch a glimpse of what hell looked like. To her surprise, it was just as Frank had described it. A perfect Utopia. She couldn't understand what the big deal was. Everyone had it all wrong. This seemed to be a great place to live out the rest of eternity. That was until she saw a busy businessman type answer his phone.

"You're going to love that if you come to hell when you die," the secretary said.

"Is, is he picking up an unwanted call from his parents?" Fran asked. Priscilla nodded. She had an evil grin. The man outside placed the phone up to his ear. He was brought to his knees almost as soon as the phone touched his ear. "That seems horrible. You monsters!" She directed her frustration at Priscilla.

"The guy did it to himself. This is hell, sweety, not a vacation destination."

What did he do to deserve this cruelty?" Fran asked. Her hands shook from the thought of something like that happening to her. She realized, that without her soul, that could very well be her. There was no telling how long she had left before she could get her soul back. It was a race against the clock to earn her salvation back.

"Do you really want to know?"

Fran looked out the window. She put her hand against the glass and whispered, "You poor soul." The man seemed as though he were suffering a fate even more inconceivable than Roberto's first excruciatingly abysmal challenge. She nodded, giving Priscilla the green light to disclose this man's horrible actions. She couldn't see him as a murderer, but he was in hell after all. She just wished, no, hoped, he wasn't a telemarketer during his time on earth. All those people deserved to burn in hell for all she cared. But, something inside of her told her that even those people deserved the least bit of leniency. Fran turned to Priscilla. She could see Death regaining his composure out of the corner of her eye. She locked eyes with the secretary.

Priscilla searched her files and pulled one up with the name Adam Sanderson. Thirty-five-year-old. Survived by his father, Ronald Sanderson, and his mother Marla Sanderson. In his teens, Adam was well on his way to being recruited by one of the BIG TEN football teams, but he fell into a rough crowd of bros that discovered Bitcoin in its early stages. Adam got lucky, and his small investment yielded him a half a billion dollars shortly after investing. He became an overnight, half a billionaire. He then spent his entire adulthood selling people on the idea that Bitcoin was a solid, stable investment, and that even entire governments were adopting this form of digital currency. He managed to get his parents, his grandparents, and many other people's grandparents to invest in the digital currency until one day, Bitcoin's value fell dramatically, after being close to a hundred thousand dollars per coin. The coin had dropped to nearly fifteen thousand dollars a pop. By that point, it was too late for most of his investors. Some had even refinanced their homes in order to buy themselves at least one Bitcoin before the crash.

"Please, no more. I understand completely why that bastard is here now. He deserves every bit of that call," Fran said. Her soft eyes now turned night terror cold at the site of Adam. She grabbed two paper cups from the water cooler station. The water was tepid at best, despite it coming out of the blue spout. She walked towards Death, who was now completely back to normal. "Here," Drink this, and let's get the hell out of here." She handed him the cup.

Let's Go To The Mall.

Chapter 11:

"We are ready," Fran said. She slammed both her hands on Priscilla's desk. Death jolted at the sound. Priscilla looked up at her with a high level of disinterest. The type a child shows when a parent tries to lecture it.

"Please, get your hands off of my desk before I cut them off," Priscilla said. She pointed at an ax behind a glass pane she materialized beside her. Fran promptly took her hands off and massaged both her wrists as though the secretary had just hurt them.

"Have at it," Death removed one of his hands. Priscilla rolled her eyes.

"I'm not exactly sure what to tell you about this challenge," Priscilla said. "Roberto hasn't quite explained it to me, but he says it's going to fuck a lot of people up. His words, not mine. So, I guess, this is your chance to leave now, because."

"Yeah, yeah. We know. If we quit mid challenge, we will be stuck in it forever."

"In the future, please don't interrupt. That's so rude." The secretary said. She waved a hand with disinterestedly, and a door appeared behind them once again. This door was much different from the last. "Oh, wait. Before you leave. I guess I have to give you two this credit card. You each get five thousand dollars to spend, but you can't bring anything back with you." She handed them the card.

"Both Fran and Death were confused. The door before them very much resembled the sliding glass doors at most indoor mall entrances. However, the other side appeared to be a blank room, just like the one they had just been in. Fran looked at her plastic card. The numbers on it were all sixes. It was a blue American Express card that belonged to Lucifer Morning Star and had the name of his LLC. Hell LLC.

They crossed the threshold into the bright white room. The doors behind them de-pixilated. The room fell silent. Enough for her to hear her heart beating in her chest. She could hear the blood slowly traveling across her arteries and veins. Her thoughts were loud with images of unimaginable fears, and unforeseen tortures that could await them. She braced for cruelty as it was provided to her not long ago, in that very room.

"Hours passed, and, still, nothing. Death laid on his back. "I'm soooo bored!" he writhed in boredom. "Maybe they forgot we were in here," he said.

"I doubt it. This must be part of their evil plan," Fran was skeptical.

"Are you kidding me? No. This is too easy. They're fucking with us," Death said.

The double doors re-pixilated. "I'm so sorry, guys. We had some technical difficulties with the equipment, but it should all be in tip-top working order now. Enjoy," Priscilla said. She quickly exited the void before Fran could address her. The sliding glass doors de-pixilated once again.

A low hum reverberated the room. Fran and Death could feel the soft vibrations against their feet. The lights flickered several times. Then, a loud beep attacked their ears for approximately two minutes. The space around them struggled to stay lit as a dome of grid of green grid squares populated the walls around them. The room fell dark. The grid squares continued flickering. Death reached for Fran. "Hold me," he whispered. Fran reached to grab his boney friend, but a mobile kiosk with oversized wooden wheels materialized between them as it surfaced from the earth. Death slammed his face against it. Fran avoided getting hurt just in the knick of time.

Soon, kiosk after kiosk materialized before them in an endless walkway full of bored kiosk people selling things, from magic orbs to fake jewelry that was advertised as pure gold. Store fronts emerged as well. Build a Bear, then a Victoria's secret, then a men's store claiming to have a doctor on site that discretely provided Viagra. Before they could process what was going on, an entire food court materialized on the second floor. The smell of free sample Chinese food flooded Fran's senses. She hoped that maybe she could get a sample of orange chicken before anything weird happened.

Death nearly floated away towards the smell of food, cartoon style. The smell of delicious Indian cuisines made Death's mouth water. Last of all, people faded in and out slowly. The entire structure crawled with life once the people stopped glitching in and out of existence. With them came the overwhelming sounds of hundreds of people talking over one another.

"Where are we?" Death asked.

Fran knew exactly where they'd been placed. The sense of dread pulled at her with the weight of a thousand really heavy objects. The all too familiar hot topic, and only brat stores were a dead giveaway. She quickly looked for a hole to crawl into. "The mall in my hometown," she said. Her voice quivered.

"What's so bad about the mall? There's so much to do." Death pointed at all of the stores. He held the credit card in front of Fran's face, dangling it as though she were a fish, and he held the bait.

"Move, move!" she shoved Death out of the way with the force of a professional defensive sports player. Death wondered how such a small girl could be so strong as he stumbled backwards.

"Francine!" Fran heard from across the way, and over the sound of hundreds of other voices. Her heart sank. She recognized the cracking, mid puberty voice even if she were blind and couldn't see who the voice was coming from. "Wait up! I've been trying to call you at home, but your parents always answer and tell me you're studying, which I thought was odd because I've never seen you open a book to save your life." The comment didn't quite come off the way he'd intended.

Fran rolled her eyes. She took a deep breath. The name finally registered in Death's mind.

"Ha! Francine!?" he laughed hard as he maneuvered his way toward her through a crowed of overweight teenagers.

"Shut up!" She told Death.

"What?" the boy said. "I didn't-"

"Not you, Scott, sorry," she said. She bickered with Death quietly. The boy looked at her, confused.

"Should I come back later?" he asked. He then motioned at a random store. "Because if you really don't want to."

Fran interrupted again. "It's fine. How are you?" Her voice sounded pseudo friendly, but her body language screamed, *get me the hell out of here!* She nervously played with her hair. Scott saw it as a form of flirtation, when really Fran had resorted to self-soothing as a result of a lifetime of frustration.

"Yeah, great to see you too," she said. Death motioned as though he was telling Scott to get on with it.

"You look amazing," Scott continued. Meanwhile, Fran had been wearing the same simple outfit for the better part of two days. She could smell her body odor escaping her pits. Her hair was greasy and unkept. She felt nothing close to amazing.

"Okay, bye!" Fran said.

"No, wait. I just wanted to know," he started. His face looked clearly hurt.

"What?" Fran barked.

"Why did you break up with me?" Fran looked at him in disbelief. Death burst into laughter. He nearly fell over.

"Yeah, Fran, why did you guys break up?" Death asked.

"Fran smacked her forehead with an open palm. "My god, not now, Scott," she said.

"If not now, when? Fran? I keep replaying our relationship in my head over, and over, and over again, but

I can't seem to pinpoint where I went wrong!" Scott started to cry.

Fran looked around her, embarrassed. She fought Scott's stroke inducing please for closure. Death plead alongside Scott for an answer. She kept from shoving him in efforts to preserve her self-respect, and not looking like a crazy woman.

"Scott," she said. He leaned closer. Fran stepped a step further. Without meaning to, Scott's expression looked even more crushed. Fran looked at the floor. The guilt had built up long enough. Scott waited silently for an answer.

"Do you want me to just claim him?" Death asked her. Fran glared. He simply lifted his palms as if to say, "okay fine, I won't."

I just. I'm not sure how to tell you. So, I'm just going to go ahead and say it. I hated how you were into Magic the Gathering so much. I mean, like at an obsessive level. From the looks of it, nothing has changed. You're wearing a Magic the Gathering shirt!" The guilt melted off of her chest. Scott, however, looked devastated.

"You bitch!" he huffed and puffed. To Fran's defense, he was wearing a hat that matched his shirt. "It's a good thing we broke up. I can't believe you. You. You monster!" Scott stormed away.

"That's normal adult behavior," Death mocked. Fran stood, unmoving. She was speechless. The corner of her mouth twitched in disbelief. She waited and followed Scott with her eyes until he disappeared into a thick crowd of mindless mall walkers.

"What just happened?" She asked Death.

"I think he realized you weren't the girl he thought you were." Death giggled. He followed an elderly couple that appeared to be no younger than a hundred years old. He looked at his death book to see if he could claim them, but they each had a solid thirty years left before he had to pay them a formal visit.

"But I'm such a catch. I'm cute, and I'm super nice," Fran mumbled. Death had come back just in time for him to hear that.

"A real cath. You're a twenty-five-year-old Starbucks barista who doesn't believe in college."

"I'm on track to becoming a shift manager."

"Does it come with a raise?"

Fran looked uncomfortable. "No, just more responsibility, and the possibility of a raise in six months." Death looked at her, almost in pity. "Oh fuck. I see my freshman year teacher, Mis Laney." She ducked behind Death.

"What good's that going to do? She can't seem me," Death said.

"Run. Run!" Fran lost sight of her old teacher. She bolted toward the stairs as she tried everything in her power to avoid the cranky math teacher.

"Franny! Oh, is that you? You look so, malnourished." Laney's face showed clear signs of concern.

Fran laughed nervously. Oh, hi Mis Laney. It's so great to see you. I so don't remember how you always told me I wouldn't amount to anything," Fran blurted. Death walked away in embarrassment. Mis Lany, however, leaned in further.

"I can't believe you still remember that," she said. Her face turned red with shame. "That was just me finding ways to inspire you young kids," she continued.

"I was definitely inspired. I'm an overworked, and underpaid barista," Fran said. The awkwardness around them was palpable. "I'm sure you're happy to see how right you were."

"At least you're not homeless?" Fran's former teacher said. She looked at her watch. "Ope, looks like I'm running late for my, um," she said and walked away.

"Kill me, please!" Fran told Death. His face lit up brightly. "Not really, you jackass. If I have to see someone else I know from my hometown, I'm going to murder everyone in this bitch," she said. Death then pointed at her mother approaching quickly.

"Fran!" Fran's mom shouted from across the mall. Fran retreated slowly into herself.

"I love your mom! I wish she could talk to me too!" Death said giddily.

Fran's mom's face began to glitch. At some moments, her face blinked in and out of existence. In others, her entire body shape shifted into unrecognizable shapes, or people. A glitch in the matrix followed her mom's malfunction. The mall went in and out of focus. The white void slipped in and out, trading spaces with a rapidly disintegrating mall scenery. Soon, the smell of smoke followed, causing the entire simulation to malfunction and turn off. As disconcerting as it was, witnessing her mother shape shift into a million different things, Fran was happy that she didn't have to explain to her mom why it was that she was still single.

A fire broke out on the far side of the void, which made it look as though it no longer expanded infinitely. The charred walls allowed them to have a better perspective. Turns out, the seemingly endless expanse of open void was no bigger than about a hundred square fee, and it was on fire.

The fire alarm blared with the intensity of a million blow horns. Red flashing lights surrounded them as Priscilla peaked her head in through the now materializing glass double doors. She pushed them open forcefully. They'd been shut down to prevent an electrical fire on the only exit.

"Looks like you guys passed the challenge. Now quickly, but in orderly fashion, exit the room. Your waivers don't include a clause in the event you die from a fiery death."

Self Care.

Chapter 12:

"That counts, right? We nearly just died," Fran asked. She was on the verge of a mental breakdown. She could handle the thought of burning alive in a wanna be endless void, but being forced to interact with people, especially people she hated, was equivalent to being ripped apart, piece by piece, and being fed to angry gremlins while being refused the sweet relief of anesthesia.

"You didn't complete the challenge," Priscilla said.

"There was no challenge to complete! The whole place literally burned down with us in it." Fran stood her ground. Her near child-like appearance made it that much more impossible to be taken seriously.

"You're so cute when you're mad," Priscilla said. She was almost genuine. Fran got even more flustered. She looked at Death for support.

"She's right," he said. He seemed a hundred percent more composed now than he did after the first challenge.

"You're no help."

"I didn't come to help you in the first place," he said. Frans frustration grew deeper. Frank just punched me without asking what I was doing," he continued.

"I wish I could punch you right now," she shoved him, half playfully. Death swatted at her like a cat. She swatted back. They both tried their hardest to move their faces away from the swattage. Frank kicked him on the shin. He laughed at her and took her into a headlock. He swirled a large was of spit in his mouth. Priscilla looked at her phone as Death put his index finger in his mouth. Fran struggled to get out of his grasp. Her hair became even messier.

"Okay, cut it out you two!" Priscilla commanded. Death stopped short of giving her the wettest we willy a celestial being had ever given.

"I hate to say it, but I like you two," the secretary told them. Her grainy voice took hold of the room. "I'll throw you a bone." Fran struggled to not make a joke about her having a heap of bones standing right next to her but decided that was most likely not a good time to make jokes. She was not about to joke as the woman holding on to the fate of her soul was about to practice a small amount of leniency.

All Fran could do was smirk, and stand still, despite every ounce of her self-control screaming at her to make a joke.

"I swear to God, I you tell Lucy I was nice I will kill you in the most painful way I can imagine." Fran and Death said nothing. They moved nothing but their eyeballs and gave each other an implied high-five.

"You're right. This wasn't your fault, and you did alright at the challenge," Priscilla said.

"So, so?" Fran blurted loudly.

"Not now!" Death angry whispered as he reached for her shoulder. Fran tried to shake him off as though she were trying to lunge at Priscilla.

Priscilla looked at both of them as though regretting her inclination toward kindness. She lifted a stack of paperwork and combed through it. She placed it down. Her high heel tapped against the pinewood floor. She liked pinewood because she could smell the hint of pine every so often. She usually caught a whiff of it at just the right time when she most needed it. She sucked at her teeth.

Death's attention began to wane. Fran began to wonder what was going to happen next. She realized she had forgotten to call in to work and let them know she wasn't going to be in for a couple of days. Then remembered she really didn't have much time to make arrangements, nor did she care if she lost that job.

"Here's the thing," Priscilla broke the silence. Death was now lost in his own thoughts. Fran narrowly escaped the space train herself. "Roberto just emailed me." She paused.

"And?" Frank asked.

"The whole system had to be shut down. You know, because of the whole fire thing not being good friends with technology and all." Fran nodded. Her expertise in anything technical could not but agree on the fact that most technological items could not see eye to eye with high temperatures. "So, this is what I'm going to do. Per the Devil's instructions, and after checking your records," Priscilla said without an once of haste. Fran's nerves stood on end. The anticipation was killing her. "Your profile says you've had a hideous growth that you've been ignoring for about five years now."

Fran was taken aback. Quite frankly, she was straight up offended. "I'm sorry? What growth?" She understood that her nose was too big for her face. She always felt a little self-conscious about it, especially since her niece told her her nose was too big for her face back when she was twenty, and her niece was six. One thing was being insulted by a little girl. It was entirely different when a grown ass demon woman had the audacity to bring it up. Fran touched her nose gingerly. Death winced. He was well aware of Fran's feelings about her nose.

"Huh? Not your nose. Really?" Priscilla clarified. "That disgusting thing is a mole on the back of your left shoulder."

Fran sighed in relief. She pulled back the tears that were beginning to form. "Oh that. Yeah. I have a pretty good feeling it's skin cancer," she said with a nervous laugh.

"That damn thing is going to kill her!" Death chimed in.

Pricilla's phone rang. "Priscilla speaking." She raised a frail looking index finger at them. "No sir. They aren't done yet. Roberto's rig? On fire sir. "She motioned what may have been an I'm sorry at them. "I'll make sure to send him in, sir. Because it's his day off, and he can't come in until tomorrow sir. Yes sir. I know. It's a disaster.

Okay. I'll let you know when they've completed this last task and send them over. Mhm, okay, goodbye."

Death got distracted by the window. The busy businessman remained crying in the fetal position. "Poor, poor soul," he said to no one. "That's why I never got involved with crypto," he added. Both Fran and Priscilla looked at him in disappointment. He looked back and caught both their gazes. "What?"

"Your next challenge is to call the damn doctor and make an appointment to get that horrifying thing checked," Priscilla said. She reached for a bottle of hand sanitizer and lathered her hands with it. Then handed the phone to Fran.

Fran felt a subtle metallic taste in her mouth. Sort of how she gets a similar feeling whenever she gets pulled over by the cops. "I don't know if I can do this, Dick," she joked despite the gravity of her situation. She had issues regulating when to be funny. Not that anyone but herself thought she was funny.

"Sure, you're going through a crisis, but you still find time to call me a dick?" he said, then crossed his arms. He looked into Fran's eyes. There was no hint of her usual, annoying, sarcastic demeanor. Instead, he saw the tears of a very real, very scared woman who was normally very feisty and independent. Her eyes cried out at him. His body softened.

"You know I've been afraid of what that thing behind my shoulder could be," her voice quivered softly.

"What's the alternative?" Death asked. She'd never seen him this supportive.

"I live a life in blissful ignorance?" she shrugged.

"Then what? You die? Either from natural causes, decades down the line, or live a short life and end up right back over here? Like the man outside the window because you gave away your soul?"

Priscilla's eyes began to water from the harsh incandescent lighting, or so she claimed. She stood up to dim them, then took a seat behind them on the small loveseat. It was more than comfortable enough for one person to cozily snuggle up on.

Fran paced. She looked at Priscilla's phone as it rested on her desk. It felt as though it was taunting her with what was sure to be detrimental news. She reached for it but stopped halfway. Death rubbed her back lovingly. He'd never felt the pain he felt for anyone like this. He'd grown to consider Fran as family. He couldn't bear seeing her this way, but he was strong. If not for him, for her. However, he'd refused to ever admit his feelings to her for fear that she did not see him as family too. Regardless, his heart ached for Fran.

"What if I have cancer, and I just fucked myself because I was too chicken shit to pick up the phone?" she asked.

"Then we can figure it out together. We will never know if you are sick or not if you don't pick up the phone, though." Death made his best effort to reassure her.

Fran stood there, staring at the phone as it sat mere inches away from her reach. Her eyes swelled with tears that were nearing the point of releasing uncontrollably. She picked up the phone.

"Hello?" Fran's voice sounded small and shaky. I'd like to schedule an appointment.

They were granted permission to exit hell and step away from their challenge so that Fran could visit her doctor. Dr. Bernstein stood to her left as she sat on a thin sheet of paper atop an ancient examination table. Death stood closely to her right. He monitored the doctor's every move intently.

"So, I'm just going to number the area, and come back in a few minutes to cut into the anomaly. I'll take a small sample, which we will then test for signs of cancer," Dr. Bernstein explained. His voice was soft, yet soothing. However, it was no help to Fran. All she could hear was a muffled sound coming from the man's face.

Her thoughts brought her back to when she'd help her mom tend to her garden in the back yard as a child. "Look at your freckly shoulders. You're going to get sunburned if you keep wearing those tank tops without sunscreen I in this heat," her mother would tell her. Fran would dismiss her, as children often dismissed their parents. The act of pulling ripe old carrots out of the earth, and pretending she was saving them from the tendrils of an evil monster (the carrot's roots) was much more appealing than taking a moment to care for her young, resilient skin. She fondly remembered their family vacations at different beaches. She was just as stubborn about not wearing sunscreen then too. She liked the way the warm sun hugged her body right before tackling the beach's cool, calming waves. Never did she imagine she was going to have to worry about being a victim of such a devastating disease.

Fran and Death waited anxiously in Priscilla's office for a response. Priscilla had stepped out to take care of an urgent matter when Fran's cellphone rang. Fran wasn't expecting any calls besides the one from her doctor. She knew that the call was going to determine how she was going to live out the rest of her life. She held the phone and stared at it.

"You got this Fran," Death said.

Fran picked up the phone. She listened carefully. Her face was unmoving throughout the entire conversation, so it was hard for Death to gauge what was happening. Fran then hung up. She lowered her phone onto Priscilla's desk and stared at it a little longer. Death could tell the news was not good.

"Suck it cancer!" Fran was overwhelmed with joy.

An Audience With The Devil.

Chapter 13:

"I swear, Prissy, if this next challenge is as bd as the last one," Fran warned.

Priscilla shifted in her chair. She wiped her hands on her dress after coming back from the bathroom. "So? How did it go?" she asked.

"Excellent. Great news!" Fran said excitedly. Priscilla clapped her hands in glee.

"Now, maybe stop avoiding taking care of your health," Priscilla scolded Fran. Fran pursed her lips and looked away.

"What are you, my mom?" Fran joked.

"Nice one," Death said. He had a goofy grin. Both because of Fran's sick burn on Priscilla, and because his friend was healthier than a horse.

"Okay, lucy will see you guys now," the secretary said. She returned to bitch mode almost instantly. Priscilla pressed a large red button on her desk. This one had white letters that said, "Lucy's office," on it. A hellish door materialized behind them the way the other doors had. "He's behind that door," she said.

"What about the challenge?" Fran asked.

"Do you want to fuck around and find out? Because I don't," Death hissed. "Tell the nice lady thank you and shut up!" he continued.

"The devil has your last challenge. Now hurry. I'm about to hit overtime, and that's a big no no right now."

"I don't know what I was expecting, but it wasn't this," Fran said.

"You and me both," Death said in disbelief. "he's a lot less self-absorbed than God," he mumbled. He was surprised to see a wall of advance higher education degrees on the wall behind the Devil, as opposed to the giant painting of himself the way God had.

"God's what?" Fran asked. She was enjoying the modern, minimalist décor in the Devil's office. He even had a few nicely placed plants strewn about. She could tell they helped with the air quality around them. I've never smelled fresh air like this," she said.

"Oh, nothing," Death replied.

"Everything is so, so neat!" Fran admired the room. "The dude is hella smart," she said while pointing out all of the degrees on the wall. She'd failed to notice him sitting right in front of them as she remained in awe.

"What brings you two here?" I was just about to pour myself a nice, cold, glass of freshly pumped glacier water," the Devil said. He extended a glass. "Would you care for some?" he asked.

"Fancy," Fran whispered. It was too pretentious for Death's taste. Fran nodded. The Devil poured two immaculate cups of water. The glass sweat with cool beads of condensation. Three ice cubes clinked in perfect harmony within the cup as they floated in the liquidy nectar of the Gods. "I think I'm going to have an orgasm," she said. Her eyes shuttered. "What have I been doing, drinking peasant water my entire life," she said. She then chugged the rest. "Yup. I'm having a water orgasm," she clarified. Death cringed in disgust. Lucifer simply laughed.

I'm glad you like it," the Devil said. He was amused. "Please, guys, take a seat. You're making me nervous," he said. He gestured toward two perfectly designed office chairs that sat in front of his desk. They sat.

"How can I help you two?" he asked. Fran remained electrified with joy from such pristine water. The after shock of a water orgasm grabbed ahold of her. Her eyes rolled backwards.

Death shrugged. He breathed a long, slow breath. "Oh, I don't want anything," he clarified. "I'm here because of this maniac. She dragged me with her without my consent," he complained.

"Wait a second. Death?" The Devil asked.

"What? What did I do? I swear it came out of her," he said.

"Is that really you?"

"I think? as opposed to whom?" Death asked.

"Always a smart ass. Why didn't you tell me you were coming? I would have let you straight through without doing any of those silly challenges," Lucifer explained.

"I tried to tell your attack dog. Great gal by the way," Death said sarcastically.

"I know, right? I love her. She's the best secretary I've had in centuries. To think, I almost didn't hire her because she has a tramp stamp."

"Is that even legal? Not hiring someone because of a tattoo? Besides, how did you even find out about the tramp stamp?"

"It's hell! I make the rules. Also, you don't really want to know, do you?" Death shook his head, and so did Fran.

"Let's get down to business. I'm assuming Death here has some sort of liking toward you. Any friend of Dick here is a friend of mine," the Devil said.

"Hardy har," Death laughed sarcastically.

"Well, I was wondering if Maybe, possibly, I could have my soul back," Fran said.

The Devil Paused mid thought. "I'm pretty sure I don't have it. I'm ninety percent certain we never made a deal," he said.

"True. We didn't," she said, emphasizing the we. The Devil seemed to track what she was saying, mostly. "I got scammed by a guy named frank. I gave him my soul because I didn't realize they were real. Then, Death, little Dick here," she giggled.

"Come on!" Death said. She laughed a proper laugh now. The Devil cackled.

"Told me souls were actually real, and he said selling it or giving it away was bad juju. However, he also said that getting a loan for it was fine as long as I repaid it, and got it back before I died, and so then I asked how much mine was worth. He said ten million dollars," she attempted to make her voice sound deeper while puffing her chest. "So, I was like holy shit. I want my soul back so I can get a loan because I'm broke. Then I saw evilness that happens to people in hell and thought maybe this wasn't such a good idea. I just want to get my soul back, so I don't end up in hell, like the businessman outside of Priscilla's office. So, pretty please, can I have my soul back?" she took a big, gasping breath and batted her eye lashes. "Sounds like a lot," the Devil said. Death began to stand up and suggest they leave.

"I'll do it. Give you your soul back," he said. Death sat back down. His Jaw hung wide open.

"You will?" Fran asked. She perked up.

"Yeah. I just need one small, tiny, little, itty bitty, thing from him." He pointed at Death.

Death pointed at himself. "Me?"

"Yes, you."

"Anything! Fran jumped. She leaned over the Devil's desk.

"Wait. No, not anything!" Death leaned over the Devil's desk too but turned to Fran.

"You can have your soul back, but only if Death agrees to lose his skeletal image. He must wear a skin suit instead," the Devil said.

"Very funny. Fran, no. That's not happening," Death said. Fran gave him an evil smile. "You aren't serious, are you?" he asked the Devil. The Devil Reached for a glass box. It was small enough to fit in one hand. The glass was clear, and it showed a misty, purple colored gas swirling within.

"Whoa!" Fran's eyes immediately darted to the glass box. "Is that it?" she asked. She tried to poke it, but the Devil moved it away from her.

"Your soul?" The Devil finished her question. "It's so pretty, isn't it?" he taunted.

Death, now realizing the Devil was serious, sat back. He took a moment. Fran peeled her eyes off of her soul. I'm nothing if not for my image," Death said.

"Of course you are. A boney exterior doesn't make you who you are," Fran said innocently. She could tell this was most likely going to result in having to forget about ever seeing her soul again.

"No one ever told you to give your soul away," he told her. There was a touch of anger and resentment toward her. The Devil leaned in.

The Devil looked at Fran. "You know he's right. No one put a gun to your head and made you sign on the dotted line," he said. Fran slumped.

"He's right," Fran said. "It is wrong of me for even joking about any of this. It is not your responsibility to bail me out of this, Dick."

"So, it's settled. I'm keeping the soul," the Devil said.

"Wait," Death stopped him.

"Death, no. I'm sorry. I gave away my soul. Now I have to live with the consequences."

"She makes a good point," the Devil said. He didn't care what happened, one way or another. He derived pleasure from either outcome. On the one hand, he gained a new soul. On the other, he got to laugh at Death for the rest of eternity. Well, it's not like he didn't already do that. Death was incredibly unqualified, and bad at his job. He did it to himself really. However, having him wear a skin suit was just icing on the cake.

"I'll do it," Death said.

"No, don't."

"You don't have a say in it. Lucifer, I accept," Death said. Lucifer rubbed his hands together.

The Devil looked at Fran. "You're going to be selfish and let him pay for your mistake?" he asked her.

"This isn't fair. I'm not asking him for anything," she said.

"His fate is in your hands, Fran," the Devil said.

"Fran, it's okay," Death said. He looked at peace.

"No, Death. I hate that I've put you in this position," she said. The Devil stood. He grabbed the glass box and walked around his desk. He sat on the desk, in front of Fran. She couldn't help but notice how pristine the stitching on his suit was. The Devil tossed the glass cube at Fran, making sure it was locked before doing so.

"You can have that back. Death already agreed to take the fall for you," he told her.

Fran examined the cube. She tossed it back at the Devil.

"Death, believe it or not, you're the only friend I've ever had," she said.

"Obviously," Death made fun of her.

Choosing to disregard him, Fran continued. "In fact, you're my best friend, and I love you. My life would be so lonely without having you to bicker with. I've never been able to have a connection like that with any living person. You don't care that I'm flawed, and that I'm crazy, and you put up with my borderline abusive hazing."

"Yeah, about that." Death weighed his options. "Despite the hazing, and the abuse, I'm willing to do this for you because, to me, you're the only family I have. Most people who meet me are scared. You see me, and instead of trying to run away, or attempting to bargain with me for your life, you accept me. You push me to do better. You don't see a monster, and I don't see an abuser. Although we will have to have a chat about that later. What I see is a spicy little sister who will beat me into shape if she sees that I'm fucking up," Death explained. He looked at Fran with loving eyes. The Devil shed a single tear. It evaporated as it rolled down his face. Fran shed a million tears. Her nose ran like a fire hydrant.

"I can't let you do this, Death."

"You don't have a choice. Lucifer, take my essence. Replace it with that horrible skin bag," Death said.

"As you wish," the Devil replied with a grin.

Skin Bag

Chapter 14:

Fran and Death reappeared in her apartment. Death sat on the ghost chair. Charles had gone out to attend his once monthly meeting of, "so you have trouble crossing?" where he and several other ghosts gathered to talk about why they thought they hadn't crossed into the afterlife yet, and what they thought they could do to make it happen.

"Don't look at me," Death said softly. He tried to hide his face. Fran sat on her bed. The sheets were still messy. They always were.

"It can't be that bad," she said. Albeit, she hadn't actually taken a look at his face. She wasn't entirely sure that he didn't look like a monster. "Let me see your face, you hideous bastard," she laughed.

"I'm hideous!" Death sobbed.

"Richard. Whether you're as hideous as you say or not, we are in this together," she said.

"I'm in this, "Death said. "You don't have to live like this!" he cried. He stormed out. His hood covered his face completely, except for his bright blue eyes. Fran ran behind him. "Stop!" she yelled as she exited her building. It had been raining. The streets were still wet. Steam seeped from the hot asphalt. The scent of earth perfumed their surroundings. Trees dripped leftover rain gently off their leaves.

Death stopped. The clouds above him were gray, but peaceful. His breath created a subtle appearance of smoke. She could notice something different about his figure, despite his long black robe hanging loosely over his body. He appeared fuller.

"I'm serious, Death. If it weren't for you, I would have never gotten my soul back!" she shouted.

"What's the point? You're going to go and get a loan for it anyway!" he said.

Fran caught up to him. "No, I'm not. I realized something. Back in hell," she said.

"What was that?" he asked.

"I don't want to end up next to that crypto bro as we ugly cry together." Death laughed. "You said it yourself; we are family. We will always have each other. Now take off that stupid hood. It's going to be okay."

Death hesitated. He slowly lowered his hood.

"Woaaah!" Fran said in disbelief.

"Just tell me. I'm hideous. Aren't I?"

A random woman walking her dog took a double take at Death. She whistled a whistle that indicated she had the hots for him. "Turn around, pretty boy! Let momma see those buns!" she said.

"See! You're drop dead gorgeous!" Fran said.

"Wait," They both said in unison.

"She can see you?"

"She can see me?"

About the Author

Hello, and thank you for reading. A little about me. As I may have mentioned, this is my first book. I'm super excited to have finally finished. It has been my goal to write a book since I can remember having memories. It all started with fan fiction about Dragon Ball Z when I was about nine years old. I'd have to sneak in episodes because my mom wouldn't let me watch violent shows, but she'd let me watch the first Exorcist movie. I'm still traumatized by it. Even thinking about it right now gives me goosebumps. Part of the reason It has taken me 33 years to write a book, in all honesty, is because I've been lazy. Most of it, though, is because I can't sit still. That, and between working long hours trying to help people make movies and T.V shows, oh and being a parent, and a husband, I have not had much time to write. I have the great writer's and actor's strike of 2023 to thank for allowing me the time to sit down and get my pen to paper. Also, I was going crazy with not being able to work, so I figured it was probably healthy to put my mental capacity (the very small amount of it I had) into something productive. I hope to get started on my second book. It will involve Fran and Death. I have some pretty good ideas as to where their antics will take them. Okay. Thanks again for reading.